19791A

The
Funding of Public and
Academic Libraries

The Critical Issue for the '90s

Alphonse F. Trezza
Editor

A CONFERENCE SPONSORED BY THE FLORIDA
STATE UNIVERSITY SCHOOL OF LIBRARY AND
INFORMATION STUDIES AND THE CENTER
FOR PROFESSIONAL DEVELOPMENT AND
PUBLIC SERVICE

G. K. Hall & Co.
New York
Maxwell Macmillan Canada
Toronto
Maxwell Macmillan International
New York   Oxford   Singapore   Sydney

G. K. Hall & Co.
Macmillan Publishing Company
866 Third Avenue
New York, NY 10022

Maxwell Macmillan Canada, Inc.
1200 Eglinton Avenue East, Suite 200
Don Mills, Ontario M3C 3N1

Macmillan Publishing Company is part of the Maxwell Communication Group of Companies.

Library of Congress Catalog Card Number: 92-4513

Printed in the United States of America

printing number
1 2 3 4 5 6 7 8 9 10

Library of Congress Cataloging-in-Publication Data

The funding of public and academic libraries : the critical issue for
    the '90s / Alphonse F. Trezza, editor.
        p.   cm.
    "A conference sponsored by the Florida State University School of
Library and Information Studies and the Center for Professional
Development and Public Service."
    ISBN 0-8161-1994-5 (alk. paper)
    1. Public libraries—United States—Finance—Congresses.
2. Libraries, University and college—United States—Finance—
Congresses.   3. Federal aid to libraries—United States—
Congresses.   4. Library fines and fees—United States—Congresses.
5. Library fund raising—United States—Congresses.   6. Libraries
and state—United States—Congresses.   7. Library finance—United
States—Congresses.   I. Trezza, Alphonse F.   II. Florida State
University.   School of Library and Information Studies.
III. Florida State University.   Center for Professional Development
and Public Service.
Z683.F834   1992
021.8'3'0973—dc20   92-4513
                                                              CIP

The paper used in this publication meets the minimum requirements of American National Standard for Information Sciences—Permanence of Paper for Printed Library Materials. ANSI Z39.48-1984. ⊚™

Contents

Contents

Preface

The Ninth Annual Library Conference, sponsored by the Florida State University School of Library and Information Studies and by the Center for Professional Development and Public Service, was held March 10–13, 1991, on the Florida State University campus in Tallahassee, Florida. The conference was planned and coordinated by Prof. Alphonse F. Trezza with the assistance and participation of Dr. F. William Summers, dean of the School of Library and Information Studies at Florida State University, who opened the proceedings. In a year of budget cuts and state government downsizing and right sizing, the topic of the 1991 Library Conference was, appropriately, "The Funding of Public and Academic Libraries: The Critical Issue for the '90s."

Randall G. Holcombe, professor of economics, Florida State University, delivered the keynote address on March 10. Dr. Holcombe's speech, "Library Funding and the Concept of Federalism," served to focus the attention of the audience on the varying levels of government funding. Holcombe detailed the advantages of both private and public provision of library service. He defined information as a public good and therefore a reasonable recipient of local, state, and federal funds but he suggested that when the federal government becomes involved in funding an institution it also seeks to control that institution. Holcombe argued that federal funds should not be used to finance public libraries; funding should occur at the local and state levels with the primary source of funding coming at the local level where the constituency can weigh the cost and benefits of providing library service.

FEDERAL FUNDING OF ACADEMIC AND PUBLIC LIBRARIES

The theme of the Second General Session was "Federal Funding of Academic and Public Libraries." Nancy C. Kranich, director of Public Services, New York University Libraries, addressed ways to use federal funds and looked at the opportunities for securing such funds. Kranich gave five reasons for federal government support of academic libraries:

1. To share scarce resources across state lines
2. To preserve and collect rare resources
3. To equalize funds
4. To provide services that wouldn't otherwise be available
5. To train professionals

Government money for libraries has decreased due to higher deficits, shrinking funds, and stiffer competition. All these factors point to the necessity of libraries becoming more politically active to secure their share of federal funds. Kranich stated that education has traditionally been a state and local concern, but she added that opportunities do exist for the use of federal monies for specific projects. Kranich ended with some suggestions for developing and utilizing political clout. Libraries must be more competitive. They must make use of the media and be specific and relevant. Proposals must be compelling, dramatic, and personal.

Eileen D. Cooke, director of the Washington Office of the American Library Association, focused on techniques for obtaining federal funding for libraries. Increasingly, libraries are being seen as less than essential. Fire departments, water and sewage facilities, and schools are competing with libraries for funding. Cooke suggested that categorical aid is the best way for libraries to compete for money. She also emphasized the need for libraries to become more politically involved in order to show that they are a vital part of the educational process and the economy.,

Ronald Dubberly, director of the Atlanta-Fulton Public Library, Atlanta, Georgia, addressed the necessity of shifting paradigms in the library world to enable us to provide better service to a larger clientele. Dubberly argued that there is a paradox within the library profession, namely, that "much of what we value as being good prevents us from being better. Things that work for us in some ways limit us in others." The current paradigm of the library world focuses professionally on organization, acquisition, and service. The institution emphasizes local ownership or proprietorship. The government has very clear divisions: Local government provides funding, administrative control, and sets policy; the state government ensures competence in terms of fiscal management, facilities, and certification; the federal government provides resources beyond the daily needs of the library. Dubberly stated that a paradigm shift is needed to develop new solutions. He recommended a new paradigm that reflects the industry of libraries: information idea transfer. The new paradigm would include planning for public library service on the macrolevel; the idea that access is not acquisition; the unbundling of services; system sharing rather than interlibrary loan; and the need for a new partnership of government and libraries. The government would take on a new set of responsibilities. Local government would be responsive to local needs, policy, priorities, and service delivery. State government would provide oversight, planning of library services statewide, and ensure both competence and minimal service levels. The federal government would provide leadership and funding, research and development, standards, models, and demonstrations, and assist in developing technical standards. The federal government needs to shift its role from one of support to one of leadership.

STATE FUNDING OF ACADEMIC AND PUBLIC LIBRARIES

The Third General Session was moderated by Lorraine Summers, assistant librarian, State Library of Florida. She addressed the issue of state funding. Barratt Wilkins, state librarian, State Library of Florida, spoke on the issue of "State Aid to Libraries in the National Perspective." He outlined the evolution of the state library from its nineteenth-century beginning as a library for the state legislatures to its present concerns of overseeing state aid to libraries and providing support. Wilkins suggested that state aid may prove to be an endangered species within the next ten years. State funds, much like federal funds, have become increasingly soft and fluid.

Ralph E. Russell, director of the Pullen Library, Georgia State Library, addressed such questions as: What do academic libraries need and what are they likely to get? Russell asserted that state support for academic libraries should be aimed at their cooperative efforts. Library networks that address resource sharing, cooperative collection development, training and staff development, and storage facilities for infrequently used library materials should be encouraged. State funding should be a stimulus to such networking and cooperation. Russell extolled the network of Alabama's Academic

Libraries and Illinet as two statewide networks that have worked to improve access and develop better services.

James M. Wheeler, director, Volusia County Public library, Daytona Beach, Florida, provided extensive information on that state. Wheeler cited some disturbing statistics. Florida has a 29 percent high school dropout rate and ranks forty-ninth in the number of college degrees granted. He views public libraries as educational institutions. Public library users under 19 use libraries for educational purposes half the time, while one-third of the volunteer literacy programs take place in public libraries. Libraries should be relegated the same type of funding and support as schools to allow them to support their educational role. Wheeler suggested the use of state lottery money for public libraries, the use of recurring funds, and tax exempt status for Friends' fund-raising for libraries.

THE ECONOMIC IMPACT OF INFORMATION: IMPLICATIONS FOR LIBRARIES

The Samuel Lazerow Memorial Lecture was presided over by Steve Edwards, dean of faculties, Florida State University. Dr. Edwards introduced Patricia Schuman, president, Neil-Schuman Publishers, and president-elect of the American Library Association. Schuman spoke on "The Economic Impact of Information: Implications for Libraries." Information, according to Schuman, can be viewed as a resource, a commodity, an economic building block, or a public good. How we see information corresponds to the way we use information. The important question of who pays for information and who benefits from it must be addressed no matter how it is viewed. Education and economics do influence our access to information and what use we are able to make of information we receive. Schuman concluded by saying that librarians can make a difference in providing those who are information-poor with tools and resources to share in the power of knowledge.

LOCAL FUNDING OF ACADEMIC AND PUBLIC LIBRARIES

The final session of the conference on Wednesday, March 13, was presided over by Sandra M. Cooper, chief, Bureau of Library Development, State Library of Florida. Marjorie Turnbull, Leon County commissioner, Tallahassee, Florida, spoke on the funding prospective of local government. County government is unique in that county commissioners both appropriate and spend county funds. In the face of declining budgets at both the state and federal levels, fiscal responsibilities that were previously held by the state and federal government are being given to local government. Turnbull discussed the need to fund essential functions and services before nonessential services. The new Leon County Library was cited as a case of public support forcing county funding. First, he said, convince policy makers that your services are essential and, second, be willing to involve friends and volunteers in funding.

Laurence A. Miller, director, Florida International University, Miami, Florida, spoke on the relationship of academic libraries and local funding. Local funding for academic libraries has dropped from 5.05 percent to 3.75 percent of their total budget. Academic libraries are facing increasing acquisitions costs and budgets that have not kept pace. Miller focused on two areas of funding: (1) attracting a larger share of basic institutional funding and (2) exploring alternative fundraising methods. Miller argued that library fundraising must be tied to the general fundraising efforts of the institution to be effective. He also encouraged the use of other income producers, such as photocopiers, and fees for online services.

John D. Hales, Jr., director, Suwanee River Regional Library, Live Oak, Florida, focused on local funding from the public library perspective. Hales stated that 82–92 percent of the total public library budget came from local funds such as sales taxes, income taxes, real estate taxes, and special, ear-marked tax revenue. The public library must constantly justify its share of general tax revenues. Hales suggested that public libraries explore alternative funding sources such as Friends' groups, trusts and foundations, library fees, impact fees, and bond issues. He concluded by stating that libraries must do a better job of proving their worth, finding unconventional funding sources, and advocating for a share of local funding.

SANDRA D. ANDREWS
Doctoral Candidate
School of Library and Information Studies
Florida State University
Tallahassee, Florida

ALPHONSE F. TREZZA
Professor
School of Library and Information Studies
Florida State University
Tallahassee, Florida

Acknowledgments

The success of a conference depends on a number of elements: the theme selected, the caliber and quality of the speakers, the physical arrangements, and most of all, the interaction of the delegates to the speakers—in the discussion sessions and during the various social sessions (meals, coffee breaks, corridor talk, and the like).

The timeliness of the issue of funding generated vigorous participation and discussion by both the speakers and the delegates. We are pleased to share the excellent papers that were presented.

I wish to acknowledge all those who contributed toward making the conference both a program and a professional success. To Dr. F. William Summers, Dean, School of Library and Information Studies, FSU, for his continuing support and counsel; Jan R. McArthur, my graduate assistant, for the many hours she devoted assisting me in conference planning and implementation; to the Center for Professional Development staff, Dr. Mary L. Pankowski, Susan Lampman, Leanne Gregory, Deirdre Rockwell, Bryna Gordon, and Laura Pichard; and to my wife, Mildred, for her patience, understanding, and support.

Introduction: Library Funding and the Concept of Federalism

Randall G. Holcombe
Professor of Economics
Florida State University
Tallahassee, Florida

A federal system of government is an effective way of providing services because it allows a level of services to match the constituents who use them. Services that benefit a national constituency are provided by the national government, while services that benefit state or local constituencies are provided by those governments. The benefits of such a system will be discussed in more detail later. The idea that library funding and federalism are related to each other implies that government is involved in library funding. In fact, government is involved, but to evaluate the degree to which federal, state, and local governments should be involved in library funding, we must first understand why government ought to be involved in library funding at all.

LIBRARY RESOURCES AS PUBLIC GOODS

The fundamental justification for government involvement in the provision of library services is that library resources fit the economist's definition of a public good. As the economist defines it, a public good is one that allows a consumer to consume this good without reducing the consumption by any other consumer.[1] Library resources come close to this definition.

Information fits the definition of a public good very well, because once the information has been produced, there is no limit to the number of people who can use it without depriving anyone else of the information. Libraries do not contain information in a pure form; rather, they contain books, microfilm, computer databases, and other resources that hold information. If a book is checked out by one person, then other individuals are temporarily unable to use it, so books are not pure public goods. But they come close to the definition, because at any one time most books will be available for users, and once one person has made use of the book, it can be used by another person without reducing it or its benefits to the first person.

Why should the government produce public goods? The economist's argument is that if public goods are made available at no cost to anyone who wants to use them, the total value of the public good is increased. With private goods such as gasoline or shoes or soft drinks, if the good is consumed by one person, others cannot use it. The role of the market system is to ration these goods so that they are allocated to those who value them the most. But with a public good like a book, new readers can continue to use the book and many people can benefit from its consumption. To maximize the benefits of the book, it should be used by everyone who places any value on it, which implies that it should be made available without charge.

Consider the following example. Assume that five individuals would be willing to pay $10, $7, $5, $3, and $1, respectively, to read a book. If the book were rented for a $4 charge, the first three individuals would rent the book, which would be worth $10 + $7 + $5 = $22 to the renters. Since the rental charge was $4, $12 would go to the renter leaving the renters with $10 in net benefits. However, if the book were lent without charge, two more individuals could borrow it, adding $3 + $1 to the use value of the book. Thus, all users together would receive $26 in value from the book if it were lent without charge, whereas the book would only produce $22 in value if it were rented for $4. Thus, to maximize the value of the book, or any other public good, users should be able to use it without charge.[2]

If the government were not involved at all, the market would undoubtedly allow for private firms to provide library services in the same way that private firms now rent video cassettes to interested borrowers. Note that these movies are also public goods in the same way as library materials—once the movie has been produced, additional viewers can enjoy the movie without reducing the benefits to other viewers. But the argument that applies to both libraries and video rental firms is that if the materials were made available at no cost, the total benefits of the materials to the consumer would be greater. Obviously, private firms could not remain in business if they lent their holdings at no cost, so there is an argument for the government to finance video cassette rental businesses and libraries, in order to maximize the benefits.[3] Even this makes too big a distinction between the two types of establishments. A video rental business is nothing more than a library, with specialized holdings on video tape.

While other justifications for the public funding of libraries might be made, they do not hold up well under close scrutiny. For example, public funding might be warranted to provide library services to socioeconomically disadvantaged individuals. However, one would be hard-pressed to argue that the disadvantaged would be helped more by giving them better libraries than by giving them better job-training programs or better health care. One might also argue that a democratic society requires free access to information, but, in fact, most politically relevant information in today's society is disseminated through newspapers and television—in the private sector.[4] Both of these arguments are made by Wellisch and associates (1974), who include both supporting and opposing arguments in their analysis. The public goods argument seems to be on much more solid footing.

ADVANTAGES OF PRIVATE PROVISION

While the public goods argument provides a justification for government provision of library services, the provision of library services at no cost raises some problems. One problem is that it is difficult to tell how much the library's services are worth. The video rental store has an incentive to carry any title that will cover its costs, and revenues from past rentals provide a guide regarding which new titles the store should purchase. There is no such market guide to tell libraries how to value the services they provide free of charge. Thus, the library does not have a good indicator of which services should be expanded because they are valuable to patrons, and which should be cut or contracted because they use funds that would be better spent elsewhere.

Should a library subscribe to more periodicals or extend its operating hours? Some patrons will want one while others want the other, and without a market indicator, it is hard to tell how scarce funds should be allocated.[5] With regard to public goods in general, this issue was raised by Minasian (1964). The problem is considered for libraries directly by Lancaster (1977). Libraries are not totally in the dark on these issues; they take surveys and do other studies to try to design library services that meet the desires of their patrons. But these studies, which use library resources themselves, do not indicate the value patrons put on specific services, as would be the case if fees were charged.

If money were no object, every library would like to be able to provide every user with every bit of information the user wanted. But if libraries had too much money (surely that is hard for librarians to contemplate), this might result in too much information being produced. Many libraries buy every university press book that is published, which gives university presses a ready market for their wares. With such a market, university presses might publish too many books. In addition to the cost to libraries to purchase and house them, it presents additional costs to users. Library users may not always know exactly what information they need, and the more information that is produced, the harder it is to search through it.[6]

The example of university press books was not meant to single them out. Academic journals surely provide another example, but public funding of libraries is likely to increase the demand for all the materials libraries buy. As one who frequently uses the library as a research facility, the author knows firsthand how time-consuming it can be to search the literature for information, much of which is either of poor quality or duplicated in other sources. Public funding of libraries could allow the production of a greater than optimal amount of information, which might lower the value of good information.

Yet another argument favoring private provision is that people would then pay for those library services they use. Library services provided at no charge must be paid for by somebody, and since almost everyone pays taxes, almost everyone pays for libraries. Rather than forcibly taking money from people through taxation and then giving it back to them in library services, users could pay for those services they use, as they do with video rental businesses. At a minimum, this would give libraries a much greater incentive to supply those services their patrons wanted.

These are issues that must be considered if a good is allocated at no charge to users, but these problems do not negate the public goods argument that once information is produced, its value is maximized if it is disseminated at no charge. The remainder of the discussion will ignore these issues and assume that it is optimal to allow access to library materials at no charge.

THE FREE-RIDER PROBLEM AND GOVERNMENT PRODUCTION

Even presuming that free access to libraries is optimal, libraries could still be financed through voluntary contributions rather than taxes. The justification for tax financing is that if libraries tried to rely on voluntary contributions, not everyone would contribute but would use the library services financed by others. Since everyone has the same desire to free-ride, too little money would be contributed. Therefore, library users are better off if they are forced to pay through taxation, which provides libraries with the money to produce services that the users might want to finance if it were not for the free-rider problem. The free-rider problem is a standard topic of public finance; see Holcombe (1988), chapter 6.

Aside from the free-rider problem, there is little difference between this type of arrangement and a club.[7] The details of this club-type arrangement were discussed by Nobel laureate James Buchanan (1965) in his famous article on public goods. Taxpayers are all members of a group that wants the benefits of a library, but they recognize that some people will not pay for such benefits unless they are forced to. They will instead choose to consume for free. One alternative is to have the market provide the service, as with video rentals, but charging for the service means too little of it will be provided. Therefore, to receive the optimal level of service, we all are forced to pay our taxes and in exchange receive the benefits of a public library.

The argument for government funding of libraries can be summarized as follows: There are advantages to allowing library resources to be used without charge; however, such libraries can only be supported by public funding. With this argument in hand, we now turn to library funding and federalism.

FEDERALISM AND PUBLIC GOODS

The primary public finance advantage of a federal system is that it allows public goods to be financed at the optimal level of government. Goods that benefit local constituencies can be produced at the local level, while goods that benefit larger constituencies can be produced by higher levels of government. Interstate highways are used mainly for long distance travel so it makes sense to fund them at the national level. Residential roads in a local neighborhood primarily benefit those who live there, so they are financed by local government. By their very nature, libraries benefit people in a local area, so like local roads, it makes sense to finance them locally. A few libraries might serve state or national constituencies (a library at a state university, for example), which might provide a rationale for state funding. But few people will travel from, say, Louisiana to Florida to use a Florida library, so there is little rationale for having Louisiana taxpayers help pay for Florida libraries. This argues against federal funding for libraries.[8] Through interlibrary loans, it is usual for users in one state to receive library material from another. However, libraries have an incentive to share resources in this way without federal involvement because all local libraries can then provide their patrons with infrequently used resources without going to the expense of acquiring and storing them. Furthermore, borrowers could be asked to pay for materials received through interlibrary loans if it proved burdensome to the library's finances. I have been asked to pay for interlibrary loan material, and that did not seem unreasonable.

Few people would dispute that federal funding of any good or service that is primarily consumed locally will generally lead to inefficiencies, so there is good reason always to finance public goods at the lowest level of government.[9] Current literature on the economics of the subject is built largely on the foundation of Niskanen's (1971, 1975) work. But the problems of efficient government provision are compounded when the population that benefits from a program is a small subset of the population that funds it. In brief, the problem is that most taxpayers and voters know little about most of the activities of government. However, those who have much to gain from particular programs are well informed about them and work through the political process to get those programs funded. The result is that a few well-informed groups push for programs that they desire but that are funded by all taxpayers. Taxpayers in general know little about most government spending, so there is little opposition, and programs demanded by concentrated special interests end up by being paid for by everyone.

To see how the process might work, consider a library program that would cost $10 million and benefit a community of library users in Illinois. Those who work in the library industry in Illinois will tend to be well informed about the program and will push the legislature to spend the money. The cost of this program will be less than $1 per U.S. taxpayer, so no taxpayer has much of an incentive to learn about the program. Even if most taxpayers would receive no benefit from the program, it just does not pay to try to stop the expenditure of such a small amount of money. Therefore, the program has lots of political support, but no opposition. In such a political environment, the program is likely to pass.[10] This is a brief overview of an extensive literature on the problems of special interest spending in politics. Downs (1957) laid the foundation for current work in the area, and is still extensively cited. More recent models of special interest politics can be found in Weingast, Sheplse, and Johnsen (1981) and Holcombe (1985).

Library programs are not unique in this regard. Every constituency has its own needs for federal funding, and while each constituency presents those needs to the legislature, there is little incentive to organize opposition. In the 1990 U.S. budget agreement, my favorite recommended special interest expenditure was the $500,000 to renovate the birthplace of Lawrence Welk. This project received so much negative publicity that it was subsequently removed from the budget. Other projects that *remained* in the budget included $500,000 to study the effects of cigarette smoking on dogs, $556,000 to fly cows to Europe as a part of an export enhancement program, $107,000 to study the mating habits of the Japanese quail, and $49,000,000 for a rock-and-roll museum. All of these organized demands for federal funding and the lack of organized opposition to them have led to today's tremendous federal budget deficits, as every constituency competes for a part of the federal budget dollar.

The reason there is such great demand for federal dollars is that those demanding them bear only a small fraction of the total cost. With fifty states, a program that provides benefits in only one state will cost that state an average of only $1 in taxes for every $50 in benefits. If the program were funded at the state level, the state would have to pay the full $50 for $50 in benefits. Federal funding looks attractive because it is a way to get other people to pay for the programs a local constituency demands. The advantage of funding local benefits at a local level is that it makes those who advocate those benefits take greater account of their true costs.

Remember, the same people who pay local taxes also pay federal taxes. They just pay them to different governments. Federal funding actually costs more than local funding because of the overhead expenditures involved in transferring money from federal to local governments, the development of regulations, oversight monitoring, and the like. Is there any justification for federal funding of local libraries?

IS THERE A ROLE FOR FEDERAL LIBRARY FUNDING?

Most beneficiaries of libraries are those who live nearby. Following the arguments already cited, this would indicate local funding for local libraries. Libraries at the state university may benefit a wider constituency since people from throughout the state are more likely to use them, which suggests that state funding would be appropriate. But as we know most library use is by people who live nearby, the arguments suggest strongly against federal funding for libraries. To reiterate: There is little reason why someone in Texas should be taxed to pay for library services in Florida.

Arguments often given for federal financing of library programs deal with planning and coordination functions, or with the redistributive aspects of free access to library services. These arguments do not hold up under close examination.

Wellisch and associates (1974) argue that there is a federal role in planning for national support services, promoting increased system organization, promoting special education support through inter-institutional cooperative efforts, and improving services to the socio-economically disadvantaged. They give arguments (1974, pp. 232–254) both for and against these types of federal support. But libraries have every incentive to establish a coordination network on their own, without federal support. The interlibrary loan system is a straightforward example of this. Libraries have every reason to establish coordinating systems that allow their patrons to take advantage of information that is in other libraries.

Getz (1980) suggests that the federal government might have a role in providing what amounts to public good for libraries, such as cataloging services. While the argument has some plausibility, it is likely to force federal standards on local institutions; additionally, multitudes of such services are already available in the market. For example, financial information is produced by Dow Jones and Dun and Bradstreet and then sold to subscribers. Similarly, libraries can form cooperatives, or hire firms to provide services to benefit all. Getz (1980, p. 147) also suggests that these services be supported by user charges. Getz's suggestion for self-financing underlines the question: Why can't libraries cooperate among themselves without federal intervention? Cohen (1985) suggests the viability of external contracting for library services. Interestingly, she notes that federal government regulations actually can stand in the way of such contracting.

The redistributive arguments are also on weak ground. In a world of unlimited resources it would be nice to make library services more accessible to the socioeconomically disadvantaged, but there are undoubtedly many other ways that scarce resources could be used to benefit them more. Wouldn't the disadvantaged be better served with job-training programs, improved medical care, or special education programs than they would with better library programs? To suggest that the most beneficial way to spend money to help the disadvantaged is to give them better library services is implausible.

Furthermore, as Getz (1980, p. 144) notes, upper income individuals use libraries more than lower income individuals do. Free library services provided by the government go mostly to people who can most afford to pay for them, while low income individuals make much less use of library services already available at no charge. The evidence suggests that the actual redistributive effect of government-funded libraries is from poor to rich, although Getz argues that the effect is not large and that the government can offset this with other programs designed to redistribute from rich to poor.

The public goods argument that holds up the best in justifying government funding of libraries suggests that libraries should be funded primarily at the local level; the arguments in favor of federal funding are weak.

LIBRARIES SHOULD NOT WANT FEDERAL FUNDING

The foregoing arguments suggest that libraries should not receive federal funding. I would now argue that they should not even want federal funding. One must recognize that the federal government gets its revenues from people who live in states and localities. If library benefits are primarily reaped by those who live in the library's locality, why should the federal government tax the local residents, send the money up to Washington, and then give it back to the local library? It would make much more sense to tax the local residents directly for the library services that will be provided for them.

One answer is, left to their own devices, localities would not fund some programs that could be funded with federal money. The earlier analysis has shown the validity of this argument. Local governments must tax their residents $50 to provide $50 in benefits, meaning that there is a much closer correspondence between benefits and costs for locally funded programs. Any federal money that went to a local library would impose almost no costs on the locality, meaning that local residents would favor the spending even if total costs exceeded the benefits. Few of us care about costs when someone else is paying. But this is the type of system in which everyone would be better off if all programs were kept at a local level. Even though it might be a little harder to raise money for local programs, local residents would not have to pay federal taxes to pay for everyone else's local programs also.

The strongest argument against federal involvement is that federal dollars almost always come with strings attached. Federal spending means federal regulation. The costs of federal regulations are well known to anyone who has to deal with them, but they have another side effect that is often not recognized: They impose standardization on what otherwise would be a more diverse system.

One of the areas in which federal support has been argued for is coordination, planning, and system organization. But if this area is federally funded, it means that the organization will take shape according to federal guidelines. As information technology develops, there is increasing opportunity for innovative approaches to the storage and cataloging of information and to the delivery of library services. A decentralized library system gives rise to more innovative approaches to library management, whereas centralization reduces innovation and tends to replace it with a standardized system. Drake and Olson (1979) note that many attempts at innovation are frequently required to find a successful approach. Thus, an already standardized system is unlikely to be the best, and any system that encourages standardization is likely to close out some potentially successful innovations. A centralized system could try to provide incentives for innovation, but the best way to do so is through a decentralized system in which each locality has the incentive to develop efficient methods of organization. There is nothing wrong with standards when they are freely adopted. The Library of Congress cataloging system is an example. But if libraries are forced to standardize, they will be unable to experiment with potentially superior alternatives and innovation will be stifled.

At the moment libraries are not forced to use the Library of Congress system, and it is worth remarking that Florida State University has some books cataloged under the Library of Congress system and some under the Dewey Decimal system. Clearly, someone thought that it was better not to adopt any single standard.

Federal regulations have the potential to dictate how libraries are managed and to eliminate local autonomy and local decision-making. For one example, Federal Depository Libraries are required to keep all federal documents unless they can find another depository library to take them, or unless they have permission to discard them. Whether the requirement is good or bad, it is an example of the federal government dictating the procedures that libraries must follow.

The potential for federal regulation is much greater, and the foundations for almost unlimited regulation already exist in the Library Services and Construction Act of 1984. To receive funds under this act, a state is required to have a basic state plan approved by the secretary of education that shall, among other things:

> (4)provide that priority will be given to programs and projects—
> (A) that improve access to public library resources and services for the least served populations in the State, including programs for individuals with limited English-speaking proficiency (as defined in section 703(a) of the Bilingual Education Act) or handicapping conditions, and programs and projects in urban and rural areas;
> (B) that serve the elderly;
> (C) that are designed to combat illiteracy; and
> (D) that increase services and access to services through the effective use of technology. Section 351d.(b)

However the act is currently interpreted, the language of the law clearly would allow the secretary of education to disapprove a state plan based on any of these criteria. For example, the secretary could claim that the state plan does not give priority to programs that effectively use technology, or that are designed to serve the elderly.

The law also allows the secretary to terminate funds previously approved.

> Whenever the Secretary, after reasonable notice and opportunity for hearing to the State agency administering a program submitted under this chapter, finds—
> (1) that the program has been so changed that it no longer complies with the provisions of this chapter, or
> (2) that in the administration of the program there is a failure to comply substantially with any such provisions . . .
> he shall make no further payments to the state under this chapter . . . Section 351d.(e)

The point here is that new laws do not have to be written in order for federal control of library programs to increase substantially. To receive federal money, a state must have an approved state plan, and the secretary of education has broad latitude within the statute to decide if a plan is or is not in compliance. Keep in mind that such a proposal is not designed for the use of federal funds, it is a blueprint for a state's entire library system. By accepting federal funding, states have already accepted the principle that the federal government has the right to oversee the state's entire library operation. No change in the law is needed for the federal government to exercise more control over state library programs. All that is needed is a more aggressive federal administrator who, using the very vague criteria already listed, decides not to approve a basic state plan.

More federal money can only mean greater federal regulation. Libraries should not think of federal funding, because federal funding ultimately means federal control. For a few extra dollars today, libraries will be compromising their autonomy in the future.

CONCLUSION

A federal system of government works well because it allows government goods and services to be produced at the optimal level of which government is capable. Efficiency considerations dictate that the optimal level for any service is the lowest feasible level; and for libraries, there is little justification for funding beyond the local level. Some libraries may serve statewide constituencies, so there may be some justification for state-financed libraries. However, on closer inspection the justifications for federal funding of libraries do not hold up well.

Federal funding is likely to increase the number of dollars going to libraries because of the nature of the political system, but the fact that federal funding allows localities to finance programs with other people's money also reduces the incentive to spend those dollars efficiently. Those who spend the money are simply not accountable to the taxpayers as would be the case with local financing.

The lure of federal money is strong and the arguments cited are unlikely to dissuade library administrators from continuing to seek it. But even if they seek such money, they should be aware that federal money comes with federal strings attached, and that if the library system in general is too successful at getting federal money, our system of autonomous local libraries will turn into a federal library system in which all decisions are made in Washington. Library administrators trying to do what is best for their own libraries will have unwittingly conspired to produce a library system that is worse for everyone. This is but a special case of the prisoners' dilemma game in which a group of individuals, all pursuing their own self-interests, end with a result that makes everyone in the group worse off. I have written about this in a political context in Holcombe (1986).

NOTES

1. This definition is attributable to Samuelson (1954, 1955).

2. Further discussion of public goods can be found in Holcombe (1988), ch. 3.

3. Even this makes too big a distinction between the two types of establishments. A video rental business is nothing more than a library, with specialized holdings on video tape.

4. Both of these arguments are made by Wellisch et al. (1974). They include both supporting and opposing arguments in their analysis.

5. With regard to public goods in general, this issue was raised in Minasian (1964). The problem is considered for libraries directly by Lancaster (1977).

6. The example of university press books was not meant to single them out. Academic journals surely provide another example, but public funding of libraries is likely to increase the demand for all materials libraries buy. As one who is a frequent user of the library as a research facility, the author knows firsthand how time-consuming it can be to search the literature for information, much of which either is poor quality or duplicated in other sources.

7. The details of this club-type arrangement were discussed by Nobel laureate James Buchanan (1965) in a famous article on public goods.

8. Through interlibrary loans, it is common for a user in one state to use library material from another. However, libraries have an incentive to share resources in this way without federal involvement because all local libraries can then provide their patrons with infrequently used resources without going through the expense of acquiring and storing it. Furthermore, borrowers could be asked to pay for materials received through interlibrary loan if it burdened the library's finances. I have been asked to pay for interlibrary loan material myself, which did not seem unreasonable to me.

9. The modern economic literature on the subject is built largely on the foundation of Niskanen's (1971, 1975) work.

10. This is a brief overview of an extensive literature on the problems of special interest spending in politics. Downs (1957) laid the foundation for current work in the area and is still extensively cited. More recent models of special interest politics can be found in Weingast, Sheplse, and Johnsen (1981) and Holcombe (1985).

The author gratefully acknowledges helpful comments on an earlier draft from Lora Holcombe and Donna Mills. Any shortcomings of the paper remain the responsibility of the author.

REFERENCES

Buchanan, James M. "An Economic Theory of Clubs." *Economica* (February 1965):1–14.

Cohen, Nina T. "External Contracting for Library Services." In *Financing Information Services: Problems, Changing Approaches, and New Opportunities for Academic and Research Libraries*, edited by Peter Spyers Duran and Thomas W. Mann, Jr., 154–164. Westport, CT: Greenwood Press, 1985.

Downs, Anthony. *An Economic Theory of Democracy*. New York: Harper & Row, 1957.

Drake, Miriam A., and Harold A. Olson. "The Economics of Library Innovation." *Library Trends*, 28(Summer 1979):89–105.

Getz, Malcolm. *Public Libraries: An Economic View*. Baltimore: Johns Hopkins University Press, 1980.

Holcombe, Randall G. *An Economic Analysis of Democracy*. Carbondale: Southern Illinois University Press, 1985.

———. "Non-Optimal Unanimous Agreement." *Public Choice*, 48 (1986):229–244.

———. *Public Sector Economics*. Belmont, CA: Wadsworth, 1988.

Lancaster, F. W. *The Measurement and Evaluation of Library Services*. Washington, DC: Information Resources Press, 1977.

Minasian, Jora A. "Television Pricing and the Theory of Public Goods." *Journal of Law & Economics*, 7(October 1964):71–80.

Niskanen, William A. *Bureaucracy and Representative Government*. Chicago: Aldine-Atherton, 1971, 1975.

———. "Bureaucrats and Politicians." *Journal of Law & Economics*, 18 (December 1975):617–643.

Samuelson, Paul A. "The Pure Theory of Public Expenditure." *Review of Economics and Statistics*, 36(November 1954):387–389.

———. "A Diagrammatic Exposition of a Theory of Public Expenditure." *Review of Economics and Statistics*, 37(November 1955): 350–356.

Weingast, Barry R., Kenneth A. Shepsle, and Christopher Johnsen. "The Political Economy of Benefits and Costs: A Neoclassical Approach to Distributive Politics." *Journal of Political Economy*, 89(August 1981):642–664.

Wellisch, Jean B., Ruth J. Patrick, Donald V. Black, and Carlos A. Cuadra. *The Public Library and Federal Policy*. Westport, CT: Greenwood Press, 1974.

PART 1

Federal Funding of Academic and Public Libraries

Federal Funding for Academic Libraries

Nancy C. Kranich
Director of Public Services
New York University Libraries
New York, New York

WHY SHOULD THE FEDERAL GOVERNMENT FUND ACADEMIC LIBRARIES?

When most people think about the federal government in terms of libraries, they immediately think of grants-in-aid, that is, funding possibilities. If there is something that ideally could be done and would not be done within the bounds of the annual operating budget, then it is time to consider opportunities for federal grants. While the Constitution permits the federal government to provide financial assistance for such local and state services as libraries, economic and political considerations often dictate the extent to which that assistance may be offered. Hence, a positive legal environment may not necessarily result in a supportive economic or political climate for financing programs in public and private university libraries.

Since the Library Services Act, which provided funds for rural library development, was passed in 1956, librarians have recognized the benefits and potential of federal support. In 1965, academic librarians joined others in realizing such benefits with the passage of the Higher Education Act. For twenty-five years, academic libraries have received funds for building, organizing, and preserving collections, training staff, and acquiring and applying new technologies. No doubt, this support has resulted in a national information infrastructure that is far better equipped to work cooperatively to advance the research needs of students and scholars.[1]

Securing scarce federal aid is really no different from competing for scarce resources on campus. Clear rationale is necessary along with a supportive environment and availability of funds. At one time, many types of social and educational institutions were successful in obtaining support. As funds diminished, these applicants often received less. Given today's financial realities, however, it is likely that only those most needy or those that are most attractive will receive funds. In such a financial climate, academic libraries will need to make even more compelling arguments for funding if they are to win even the limited support of previous years.

Generally, the federal government funds libraries for the following reasons:

- To share scarce resources across state lines
- To collect and preserve unique resources
- To equalize the level of services to all citizens and bring facilities up to a minimum standard
- To support research and demonstration projects that can benefit a wide array of libraries
- To train professionals, particularly those from minority populations

Because education has traditionally been a responsibility of state and local governments, policymakers have tended to restrict the federal role to these areas. This contention that library support is a state and local concern was stressed by the administrations of Gerald Ford and Ronald Reagan. George Bush has continuously emphasized the importance of "a thousand points of light" for supporting social programs. Hence, in today's political and economic climate, reliance on nonfederal sources, including private funding, prevails. As a result, grant writers must recognize the importance of presenting projects that have broad appeal, far beyond the confines of their institutions, particularly when those institutions are private.

Over the same decades that priorities shifted, so did funds. The amount of dollars available for domestic programs simply shrunk. Most recently, the budget deficit and spending limitations in keeping with the Gramm-Rudman-Hollings deficit reduction targets have severely contained the prospects for even level funding let alone increases to meet the inflation rate. Furthermore, the last decade has witnessed zero funding recommendations by the president for most federal library programs, thereby leaving the profession with a hard annual fight just to restore previous funding. Unfortunately, the Bush budget recommendations follow in this recent tradition: zeros on most lines, except Title I of the Library Services and Construction Act, which would be reprogrammed for literacy programs only.[2]

Clearly, hopes for federal support for advancing national library programs have diminished over the past decade. No longer can librarians look to the federal government for funds to undertake many of the activities beyond the reach of their local budgets. Moreover, they must compete rigorously with other programs, such as the College Work Study Program, that are just as critical to their institutions and often essential to their financial stability. In sum, librarians are facing a dire funding situation at all levels that requires far more political involvement and determination than ever before. Accordingly, they will have to present a far more compelling argument for support if they are to continue offering the kinds and levels of services required and expected by the students and faculties on their campuses.

WHAT FEDERAL PROGRAMS SUPPORT ACADEMIC LIBRARIES?

For those not too discouraged or timid to apply for limited federal funds, there are numerous programs targeted for supporting academic libraries.[3] Most notable is the Higher Education Act, Title II. The four parts of this Title are aimed at assisting needy college libraries with collection development funds; training librarians and encouraging research and demonstration projects; supporting the organizing and preserving of unique research collections; and encouraging the use of new technologies. The first part, for college libraries (Title II-A), has not been funded for several years. The other parts have received fairly steady funding for the past decade. As a result, higher costs of staff and resources result in either fewer grant awards or lower funding.

Title II-B, Library Training, Research, and Development, provides funds for scholarships and projects to improve libraries. Since the grant's inception in 1966, the government has given more than 4,000 awards, mostly to members of minority groups. Approximately two-thirds of the program's annual appropriations of less than $1,000,000 goes toward these fellowships or training institutes; the remainder is targeted for research projects, very few of which can be supported in any one year.

Title II-C, Strengthening Research Library Resources, encourages research libraries to catalog and make accessible unique materials. Of the 83 applications received in 1989, 32 were funded at a cost of $5.675 million; 26 of these projects were new and the rest continuations. Funding levels have remained in the $5 million to $6 million dollar range since the inception of the program in 1978.

Title II-D, the College Library Technology and Cooperation Grants Program, is designed to encourage resource-sharing projects among the libraries of higher education institutions through the use of technology and networking. In 1989, the Department of Education received 175 applications under this grant category and awarded 52 projects, at a cost of $3,651,000. Among the grant recipients were twenty-three two-year public institutions, seven public four-year (or higher) colleges and universities, and eight non-public four-year (or higher) colleges and universities. Funding levels ranged from $26,000 to $637,000; total funding was about $50,000 higher than the previous year, which was the first year of the program.

The HEA II-C and II-D programs are the largest federal programs targeted specifically for academic libraries. Combined funding for the two programs last year represented just over half the funds used to support programs at New York University Libraries during 1989–1990. While recipients of these funds could enhance their overall annual funding picture significantly, the total contribution in support of academic library programs nationwide is minuscule and the probability of winning an award slim. Therefore, librarians cannot view these programs as substantial sources of funding, but merely seed money for accomplishing narrowly defined objectives, limited in scope and duration, for the period of the grant only.

Numerous other federal programs also provide funding for academic libraries. The Library Services and Construction Act, Title III, provides monies for interlibrary cooperation. In the New York area, Title III funds have supported retrospective conversion of serials at all types of libraries, including academic. The National Endowment for the Humanities annually provides close to $3 million for humanities projects in libraries and archives (for which one in four applicants is successful), another $3 million for approximately thirty research collection access projects, plus $19,000,000 for preservation activities and $14,000,000 for challenge grants for which libraries are eligible. An agency tied to the National Archives, the National Historical Publications and Records Commission, assists libraries and archives with collecting, preserving, arranging, describing, and publishing papers and documents of national historical significance. Made available last year was $5.2 million for approximately 150 projects with a cost range of $450 to $386,000.

WHAT OTHER FEDERAL PROGRAMS AFFECT ACADEMIC LIBRARIES?

Although the previously mentioned programs were formulated specifically to assist academic libraries, many other federal grants and services may also be applicable.[4] Probably the most influential of all federal services to the nation's libraries is the Library of Congress. With annual support of nearly $300 million from the Congress, the Library provides cataloging information at the rate of 175,000 titles, circulates 21,000,000 items to blind and physically disabled readers, preserves on microfilm nearly half of all titles filmed, lends 35,000 items through interlibrary loan, and recently began offering dial-up access to its automated databases.

The National Agriculture Library and the National Library of Medicine offer similar programs for their more specialized constituents. Agricola and Medline are just two of the important databases provided by these two libraries. NAL works closely with land-grant institutions, and NLM has launched a major initiative to encourage medical institutions to integrate their information systems. Other federal libraries also assist academic libraries with bibliographic and reference services.

The Department of Education lends aid through statistical services and administers grants such as the HEA Title VI program, which helps support the acquisition of foreign language materials. The education department also manages federal student loan and scholarship programs, most notably the College Work Study Program, which subsidizes student part-time workers hired by libraries and other campus facilities.

The federal government is the largest single publisher in the world. Through its Government Printing Office (GPO), National Technical Information Services (NTIS), and other similar outlets, libraries and the general public can purchase at low cost the results of many government research efforts and reports. GPO also administers the Depository Library Program, which distributes many documents at no cost to 1,400 libraries, at least one of which is in every congressional district.

Unfortunately, these traditional distribution mechanisms are at risk due to budget constraints, a greater reliance on the private sector for disseminating government information, and the computerization of many sources previously distributed in print formats. Although the GPO has launched several pilot projects to distribute computerized data through the depository libraries, pressure to privatize these services leaves the potential for this program in doubt.

Several legislative efforts are in progress to clarify the responsibilities of agencies relative to electronic data distribution. The Paperwork Reduction Act amendments under consideration in 1990 encouraged a wider role for the private sector. The Government Printing Office Improvement Act included depository libraries in the distribution network for computerized information. Neither bill passed; both may be considered again in the upcoming congressional session. Librarians need to familiarize themselves with these initiatives and point out the dire consequences to their users if the private sector alone obtains responsibility for distributing many important, expensive sources that the public has relied on depositories to provide. Neither the public nor academic libraries can afford to pay prices for privatized government information that may exceed the government's price by ten to twenty times.[5]

Another key area that has major fiscal and operational impact for academic libraries is the pending developments relative to Senator Albert Gore's proposal for a National Research and Education Network (NREN).[6] This telecommunications infrastructure would expand and upgrade the existing interconnected array of research networks that are known collectively as the Internet. If enacted, the legislation offers the possibility of transforming the basis of scholarly communication in the nation to a more efficient, higher-quality, speedier system that could be accessed not only through higher education institutions but also through libraries of all types nationwide. This resource could prove far more effective in facilitating access, as well as lower the cost of data communications. Librarians need to recognize the importance of this initiative and stress to their legislators the benefits of including libraries along with other scholarly institutions.

Libraries have also benefited from postal subsidies designed to promote the dissemination of information throughout the nation through free and reduced rates for certain preferred classes of mail. These subsidies lower the rates paid for book shipments, periodicals, and interlibrary loan, and eliminate charges for bräille and other special materials for blind and visually disabled individuals. Continual threats to these subsidies could result in libraries paying approximately 27 percent more for second-class periodical materials, 38 percent more for third-class fund-raising mailings, and 6 percent more for library rate book packages. Combined with the recent postal rate increases, loss of subsidies could prove quite costly to academic libraries already faced with budgetary shortfalls.

The federal government provides funding for individuals as well as programs that can benefit academic librarians along with the institutions in which they work. Training and fellowship grants are one source of support. Another is the USIA Book Fellows Programs that enables U.S. librarians and publishers to enrich and broaden their career experiences through a short period of overseas service in order to increase international understanding and promote resource sharing. A NY University librarian who went to Jordan on this program found the experience very worthwhile. Other scholarly exchanges are also available to librarians.

APPROPRIATIONS: KEY TO FUNDING

No matter the number of programs that might assist libraries, they cannot offer support without adequate appropriations. The level of appropriations for these programs in recent years has rarely exceeded previous levels. Over the past decade, the federal budget process has become the major focal point for public policy debate. The future of federal programs is now determined mostly through budget and appropriations committees, rather than through authorizing committees whose members are commonly the most familiar with and sympathetic to the nature and importance of the programs they oversee. This means that eleventh-hour debates and resolutions often dictate the level of support libraries receive from the federal government. No matter how effective the promotional efforts of librarians may have been, their fate is tied to a much larger, less controllable political process that ends up with horse trading and bargaining chips that relate little to the importance and effectiveness of particular programs and services.

If they are to succeed in securing any funding from the federal government in the years to come, librarians must be ever-vigilant and involved with the political process. The scarcity of funds translates into a far more competitive environment than previously experienced. Skills in the politics of the budgetary process are just as essential as reference or cataloging skills. No opportunities to keep legislators and their aides informed of the importance of library services can be missed. Fact sheets explaining what will be lost, as well as the benefits of previous grants, must be developed and widely circulated. Librarians must also send letters, testify at hearings, and enlist the support of users and other interest groups in order to promote their ideas and concerns. They must not ignore the media either, when launching their legislative action campaigns. The more widely known, the more apt legislators will be to hesitate when cuts are aimed at library programs. What is needed are short, concise letters with personal stories, timed to when the issue is alive. They must be specific, presenting relevant facts and figures. And they should be followed up by thank-you notes when a legislator acts on one's behalf.

SUCCESSFUL GRANTSMANSHIP

Even with funding assured for programs that support academic libraries, individuals and institutions still must compete aggressively for awards. This competition requires just as much skill and perseverance as lobbying for programs. A successful grant must be well conceived and well documented.[7] The actual proposal is not unlike a legal document. It must specify the purpose, significance, need, future results, staffing, management, cost, and timetable. The need for a project must appear serious; the better documented this need, the more compelling. The methodology must be appropriate. For example, if a library is seeking preservation funds, it must use standardized filming techniques that will survive the ravages of time. A method for evaluating the effectiveness of the project should be incorporated. Also, the budget should include adequate funding and be carefully justified in the narrative. In addition, it should represent indirect costs, even if the granting agency will not support them. It is important to show these institutional costs for overseeing the project. They may be quite substantial. Also, applicants need to show items that will be *cost shared* such as the project director and other staff involved with the project, but funded by the home institution. Many grants require a substantial amount of such cost sharing. Agencies want to see a commitment from the applicant.

Qualified people must manage and staff the project. You need to prove your credibility in terms of your ability to carry out whatever you have promised. Show why your library is the most appropriate site for this project. Generally, it is a good idea to communicate with the granting agency prior to developing the proposal. Grant officers are familiar with programs and can advise you on appropriate ways to proceed with your application. You should also ask them for reviews of previous submissions that were not funded. These reviews often highlight the weaknesses of a proposal that can be readily overcome through revisions. Finally, submit the proposal on time. Federal grants received late are automatically omitted from the review process, no matter how important.

Once a grant is approved, the applicant must fulfill several obligations stipulated by the federal agency. Often, the terms of the final contract are not exactly what was requested in the proposal. Adjustments to the budget and work plan may be necessary. Arrangements for recruitment must be made in advance if staff are to be available once the project begins. Make sure the project proceeds on schedule. Some funding is often withheld until completion of the project. It cannot always be reallocated if the end date is later than planned. Accordingly, any extensions or modifications in the project must be communicated and approved in advance by the authorizing agency. Reports should be submitted on schedule as well, with positive results of the project highlighted. It is always a good gesture to keep legislators and the press fully aware of the effectiveness of your project. This is the only way the importance of the program can translate into further appropriations and assistance in future years.

THE ROLE OF LIBRARIANS IN ASSURING THE CONTINUATION OF FEDERAL PROGRAMS FOR ACADEMIC LIBRARIES

Only those working in libraries can communicate the importance of particular grant programs to their own constituents. Only those working in libraries can determine how existing federal programs can assist their local efforts. Consequently, librarians in every academic library in the country must take it upon themselves to assure the continuation and growth of federal grant support. You must find ways to tell your stories, your successes, to the public—to your users, to your administrators, to your representatives, to the media. Only with publicity to those who can bolster your efforts will the importance of these programs ever be learned.

This is a precipitous year for federal library programs. The 1991 White House Conference on Libraries and Information Services on July 9–13 provided the perfect opportunity for librarians around the country to speak out about their services. The role of information in national productivity and in shaping an enlightened electorate is a key theme that academic librarians can focus on to demonstrate its importance. The Association of College and Research Libraries has prepared a position paper outlining the importance of academic libraries as a source of national strength, the federal role, and actions recommended to Congress; it is a worthy tool for advocacy purposes.[8] ACRL has also recommended a position on the pending reauthorization of the Higher Education Act, which was reinforced by ALA Council in June 1990.[9] This article reinforces the theme presented here, that given the current budgetary climate, strong justification is needed to continue HEA Title II programs. Support by librarians throughout the country must be heard if the programs in this Act are to be continued and strengthened to reflect current needs in libraries.

Librarians need not travel to Washington, attend Library Legislative Day, or obtain large federal grants to be visible in the federal funding arena. They can work from their offices in developing ideas for support, writing letters, contacting representatives in their home districts, and alerting the public to the importance of libraries and the threats to their programs. No one else is capable of telling your story. No one else can make federal programs happen for your libraries.

NOTES

1. For the history and rationale behind federal funding programs for libraries see R. Kathleen Molz, *Federal Policy and Library Support* (Cambridge, MA: MIT Press, 1976); and *The Federal Roles in Support of Academic and Research Libraries* (Chicago: American Library Association, 1991). Marilyn Gell Mason, *The Federal Role in Library and Information Services* (White Plains, NY: Knowledge Industry Publications, 1983).

2. Current funding proposals for library-related programs are reported regularly by the American Library Association (ALA) Washington Office in their *Washington Newsletter* and their semi-annual *Legislative Report of the ALA Washington Office*. The Association of Research Libraries *Bimonthly Newsletter of Research Library Issues and Actions* is another good source for information about federal aid programs for academic libraries.

3. Current grant programs are detailed in applications provided by the U.S. Department of Education, Office of Educational Research and Improvement. That office also publishes abstracts and analyses of projects funded annually. The U.S. Catalog of Federal Domestic Assistance is another source for grant program information. See also Congressional Research Service, *Federal Assistance to Libraries: Current Programs and Issues* (Washington, DC: Library of Congress, April 16, 1990).

4. The American Library Association Washington Office publishes a booklet entitled *Federal Grants for Library and Information Services: A Selective Guide*, which describes ninety-one federal grant programs that might benefit libraries but are not necessarily targeted directly to them.

5. For additional information about legislation related to government

information, see the American Library Association Washington Office *Washington Newsletter*, the *Coalition on Government Information Newsletter*, and the *Legislative Report of the ALA Washington Office*. See also Nancy Kranich, "Government Information: Less Is Dangerous," reprinted in *The Best of Library Literature, 1988*, edited by Jane Anne Hannigan (Metuchen, NJ: Scarecrow Press, 1989):49–58; and "Information Drought: Next Crisis for the American Farmer?" *Library Journal* 114(June 15, 1989):22–27; Peter Hernon and Charles McClure, *Federal Information Policies in the 1980's: Conflicts and Issues* (Norwood, NJ: Ablex Publishing, 1987); and Donna Demac, *Keeping America Uninformed: Government Secrecy in the 1980's* (New York: Pilgrim Press, 1984).

6. For further background, see Carol Parkhurst, ed., *Library Perspectives on NREN: The National Research and Education Network* (Chicago: Library Information and Technology Association, October 1990).

7. For advice on competing for library-related grants, see Richard Bos, *Grant Money and How to Get It* (New York: Bowker, 1980); Emmett Corry, *Grants for Libraries: A Guide to Public and Private Funding Programs and Proposal Writing Techniques* (Littleton, CO: Libraries Unlimited, 1982); Sul L. Lee, *Library Fund-Raising; Vital Margin for Excellence* (Ann Arbor, MI: Pierian Press, 1984); and Barbara Dewey, *Raising Money for Academic and Research Libraries: A How to Do It Manual for Librarians* (New York: Neal-Schuman, 1991). Also see "Fund Raising and Grant-Making Agencies," *The Bowker Annual: Library and Book Trade Almanac* (New York: R. R. Bowker).

8. See Patricia Wand, "Academic Libraries: A Source of National Strength," position paper prepared by the ACRL Task Force on the White House Conference on Library and Information Services, *College and Research Libraries News*, 51(September 1990):713–715; and David Walch, "A White House Conference Primer for Academic Libraries, *College and Research Libraries News*, 51(October 1990):849–850.

9. See Ruth Patrick, "Higher Education Act Reauthorization," position paper prepared by the ACRL Legislation Committee. *College and Research Libraries News*, 51(September 1990):716–720.

Federal Funding of Academic and Public Libraries

Eileen D. Cooke
Director
American Library Association, Washington Office
Washington, DC

Some of you may recall bygone days when there was talk of the Gramm-Rudman-Hollings Deficit Reduction Act, or GRH. The emphasis then was on reducing the mind-boggling national deficit. With the outbreak of the Persian Gulf situation in August 1991 and the buildup of U.S. military forces in that area, all thoughts of the so-called "peace dividend" (the savings from the proposed cutback in defense expenditures slated in the Fiscal Year 91 Budget) went up in smoke. As the weeks went on, talk of reducing the growing budget deficit, then around $100 billion, faded as U.S. troops were massing under the name of Desert Shield and deficit projections were mounting to over $300 billion.

Congressional leaders met repeatedly with White House staff in what was called the budget summit. Before Congress finally adjourned in late October 1991 we had the Omnibus Budget Reconciliation Act (PL 101-508) with a section called the Budget Enforcement Act (BEA). Now, instead of focusing on that monstrous deficit as the GRH deficit reduction law did, BEA featured caps on spending and walls between three divisions in the federal budget—defense, domestic, and international—for the next five years with little or no leeway for inflation. In effect, this means that all domestic programs will be competing for a shrinking sliver of the federal fiscal pie.

On February 4, 1991, President Bush submitted a $1.45 trillion budget to Congress for FY 1992, which proposes to zero LSCA and

HEA II and further reduce the ESEA Chapter 2 school improvement block grant, which includes school library resources. At first, the administration's proposal called for a 75 percent cut in the programs, stating that LSCA was too flexible and should be focused on adult illiteracy activities with a $35 million budget instead of the $143 million appropriated the year before. But in the next breath they declared that the $35 million should be consolidated with several other current programs and turned over to the governors in a block grant of $15–$20 billion with maximum flexibility to spend on their state priorities.

Now is the time to launch a letter-writing campaign. Get those letters coming in every week, especially if you have representatives or senators on the Budget or Appropriations Committees. Those of you who live in Florida have Congressmen Lehman, Young, and Smith on Appropriations. If you are not their constituents, write to your own representative and ask him or her to talk to the committee chair about rejecting the administration's budget proposal.

Tell your congressmen how you have used federal dollars in the past and what your needs are now. Tell them what you have planned to do with federal assistance this year and how it serves as seed money to help maintain local effort and attract additional matching dollars.

In promoting the value of libraries and their services, you may want to take a cue from a January 31, 1991, *Congressional Record* statement (p. E377) by Florida Rep. Andy Ireland. He said that the state of Florida was proclaiming February 1991 as "Grapefruit Month." Florida has been producing grapefruit for over 175 years, covering about 125,000 acres with more than 11 million grapefruit trees. The total economic return of the Florida citrus industry, including grapefruit, is more than $8 billion annually. Florida produces more than 50 percent of the world's supply and expects to harvest more than 4 billion pounds during the 1991–92 season.

If that proud statement leaves you puzzled, remember National Library Week, state pre-White House Conferences, and the national White House Conference on Library and Information Services. These events are all opportunities to tout the value of libraries. Let me spark some brainstorming on your part by quoting a few items from an Illinois Library Association fact sheet titled "Library Industry Economic Report":

> There are more than 2,843 school, public, academic and special libraries in Illinois.
> More than 14,156 people work full-time in libraries in Illinois and more than 10,981 work part-time in libraries in Illinois.

Collectively, Illinois library employees earned more than $363,244,796 last year. This money was recycled into other areas of the Illinois economy.

More than 89,952 Illinois citizens are dependent upon Illinois libraries for their income. Collectively, they paid more than $116,547,600 in state and local taxes.

Last year, Illinois libraries spent more than $128,996,128 to purchase books and other library materials, and more than $16,555,340 on computerized information databases. This money was recycled into other areas of the Illinois economy.

MORE PEOPLE WORK IN THE ILLINOIS LIBRARY INDUSTRY THAN IN ADVERTISING, COAL MINES, AUTOMOBILE REPAIR SHOPS AND GARAGES, OR DENTISTS' OFFICES! THE LIBRARY INDUSTRY IS A VITAL COMPONENT OF THE ILLINOIS ECONOMY . . . AS AN EMPLOYER, AS A CONSUMER, AS A DISTRIBUTOR!

In the March 7, 1991 *Congressional Record,* Sen. Paul Simon of Illinois pointed out that we are slipping behind in the education battle, according to a 1985 study of 8th graders in twenty countries. U.S. students ranked 10th in arithmetic, 12th in algebra, 18th in geometry, 9th in physics, 11th in chemistry and last in biology. In FY 1949, 9 percent of the federal budget was spent on education. Today, 3 percent is being spent on education. Sen. Simon said we have to do better and quoted President John F. Kennedy, saying, "Our progress as a nation can be no swifter than our progress in education. The human mind is our fundamental resource."

In the same statement, Sen. Simon pointed out that some people say we are first in the world in spending for education. But that, he said, is because we had done so well in the area of higher education but now we are falling behind. Student aid has gone down an average of 3 percent. And when you take away the higher education factor, the United States drops to 14th place worldwide in our support of education. Meanwhile, we hear that twenty-three million American adults are functionally illiterate and that four million of them cannot read their own names in block print. Simon went on to applaud the fact that the nation's governors and the president have endorsed the Goals for American Education. He concluded by saying, "If we are slipping in education, we are slipping as a nation. We can do better and we have to do better."

During the thirty-four years we have had categorical support for library programs, beginning in 1956 with the Library Services Act, and moving on to 1965, with Title II of the Elementary and Secondary

Education Act for school library resources and Title II of the Higher Education Act for academic library resources and training and research and demonstrations, nearly $4 billion has been appropriated to carry out these programs. Fortunately, we have had the benefit of solid bipartisan support in Congress for libraries, despite a series of attempts to eliminate the programs and turn them back to the states. Once again, the administration is claiming that LSCA and HEA II have accomplished their mission, federal aid is no longer needed, the states and localities can carry on without it.

At the same time, a clarion call is going out across the land to help eradicate illiteracy, to keep kids in school, to make United States students first in the world in science and mathematics achievement. If we are going to meet these goals, libraries and librarians must have federal assistance to spur their states and communities on, despite their own staggering deficits. Libraries are a part of this nation's infrastructure and they are contributors to its economy. With parental participation and the benefits of preschool story hours. In "America 2000, an Education Strategy," goal 1 states, "By the year 2000, all children in America will start school ready to learn." Goal 5 says, "By the year 2000, every adult American will be literate and will possess the knowledge and skills necessary to compete in a global economy and exercise the rights and responsibilities of citizenship."

Paradigms, Paradox, and Possibilities: The Role of Federal Funding in an Effective Public Library Future

Ronald A. Dubberly
Director
Atlanta–Fulton Public Library
Atlanta, Georgia

For public libraries the future does not look rosy. Further, that future probably will become much worse than we now believe likely, unless fundamental positive changes occur. Fortunately, there is reason to believe that these critical changes can happen. It is possible that the future for our nation's public library services can be improved.

This paper explores three primary areas:

- Critical barriers to future public library effectiveness
- Key changes required in professional focus, institutional emphases, and the funding roles of government
- The necessity for federal activism through greatly increased and direct funding for "compensatory library service" and federal leadership in public library services research and development

The critical barriers and key changes discussed here are essential aspects of the current landscape of public library service. As such, they are integral parts of the context in which the federal funding role for public libraries operates. Their nature and impact on public library service are intertwined with that of government funding roles. Therefore, any reconsideration of the federal funding role for public libraries must include all three facets.

FUTURE SERVICE DELIVERY POSSIBILITIES

The following vignettes illustrate some of the possibilities for effective future public library service possibilities. Each scenario presupposes new paradigms about professional focus, institutional emphases, and government roles.

Rural Free Delivery

A woman drives into a very small rural town, parks, and enters the hardware store. She says good morning to the proprietress and approaches an ITM. Its console includes a computer keyboard, video screen, and printer. Using the menu displayed on the screen and the keyboard, she first inquires about a novel published in 1945, recently mentioned by her mother. She requests that it be sent directly to her farm home. Next, she inquires about the topic of "county government" and identifies a magazine article on effective elected county officials. A printout is requested and received while she is at the console. The article will assist her first campaign for public office. Then, concerned for her crop, she asks for information on pine beetle control. The image of a federal document appears on the screen. She reads the brief document and learns a prevention strategy using a safe biodegradable substance. The product is purchased at the hardware store. She leaves the store for the courthouse elections office, the next stop on her itinerary.

Service Partners

A young mother is attending classes in an urban job-training center to improve her skills. She wants to get and keep a better job. After class, she walks down the hall and enters an office. While waiting briefly for assistance from the information aide, she examines several brochures on interviewing skills. After explaining her needs to the information aide, she is seated at an ITM console where she consults a menu-driven database on currently available jobs. Quickly, she obtains a listing of positions available within her zip code area. The list is printed for her.

Next, she asks for information on household budgeting. Again, the ITM is used. Soon, a videotape and a book are identified. She inquires about the availability of a VCR. Arrangements are made for her to use one at the office the next day, when the tape is delivered. The book will be sent directly to her home.

New Business

A manufacturer's representative has added a new line of products to her portfolio. Now she needs to identify a new set of potential customers. She turns on the PC in her home office. Dialing into the public library's electronic information center, she consults two databases. One is commercially produced and the other is a locally generated database. She combines information from the two databases into a working file within the library's computer. Using its software, she manipulates the data. Next, she downloads into her PC the precise information she is seeking about selected businesses in her sales territory. She is ready to make her calls.

INGREDIENTS FOR AN EFFECTIVE LIBRARY FUTURE

The above vignettes are glimpses into an effective public library service future. However, to make these and similar stories commonplace, several key changes are required. The ingredients for these prerequisites include:

Information and documents available in electronic format

Public library hardware and software compatible with those used by businesses and individuals

Networks of electronic catalogs and data bases

Efficient delivery of documents to homes and offices using fax, downloading to user computers, and physical delivery

Professionally trained staff (in addition to trained professional staff) skilled in interpersonal and electronic communication, reference interviews, and PC use, and knowledgeable about the availability and use of materials and databases

New and varied kinds of spaces for service delivery

Shared systems and *shared* users

LIMITING VIEWPOINTS

All of these conditions are feasible. Some are already available in individual public library systems and in networks serving a number of public libraries. Then why is such public library service not commonplace today? Why is such service not likely to occur soon for most users?

One primary reason is that, generally speaking, public librarians and public libraries think about and develop *cooperative* systems rather than *shared* systems. There is a world of difference between the two concepts. Cooperative systems allow access into other systems from a user's assigned system, after the user has worked through one or more protocols. Most interlibrary loan systems are examples of cooperative systems.

A shared system for ILL would provide for users either a union card catalog or an on-line catalog with a transparent electronic gateway. The users from any sharing library would receive items requested without dealing with issues related to their status at other institutions. All users would be treated the same as primary clients of the holding library's institution. As important, all users would find institutional boundaries barrier-free in terms of access ease. An effective future for public library services presupposes shared electronic catalogs, databases, and delivery systems and shared users.

LIMITING VALUES

Clearly, a change in conceptual thinking is required for the full development of shared systems and shared users and other preconditions for an effective public library service future. The development of this future is inhibited by some of the values held in public library circles. A successful future is inhibited by the very paradigms that have enabled public libraries to become what they are today. Without major conceptual changes, the possibilities presented by the three vignettes are not likely to become commonplace because some of the very values that have guided public libraries through past decades now limit their futures.

Three sets of values have been, are now, and continue to be extremely important in establishing the direction and health of public libraries. These three value sets provide focus for our professional librarians and their associations, regulate the emphases of public library institutions, and help determine the roles played in public library support by local, state, and federal governments. The values associated with these topic areas are embedded in the major concepts used for thinking about public libraries and their services.

THE PARADOX OF PARADIGMS

Together, these concepts form a paradigm or *mental map* about the institution and services of public libraries. Paradigm, as used here, can be described in the words of Stephen Covey (1989, p. 23) "to mean a model, theory, perception, assumption or frame of reference. In the more general sense, it's the way we 'see' the world—not in terms of our visual sense of sight, but in terms of perceiving, understanding, interpreting."

The paradox about paradigms is that the very paradigms (mental maps, world views) that enable us, at the same time also limit us. Much of that which has been held dear to the discipline of librarianship, to public libraries as institutions, and for the roles of government in supporting library services also prevents public librarians from being more effective professionally, prevents public libraries from providing better library service, and impedes government in providing greater availability and superior use of public funds. Some of the concepts that have allowed public libraries to survive until now may also prevent them from being successful tomorrow.

What is restrictive in our mental map about public librarianship, public libraries, and government roles in funding library services? What in our frame of reference seems good, but in reality is contrary to the best interests of future public library service?

Which dearly held values are holding back public library service? Which priorities of profession, practice, and government participation are inappropriate or improperly used? What are the models and formulas we use today that are not solving old resistant problems?

PUBLIC LIBRARIES' LIMITING PARADIGM

The generally held paradigm for public library service, today, is based largely on a highly structured theoretical organization of knowledge used for an analogous arrangement of as many physical items as can be acquired for ownership and stored within as large a facility as can be financed by the smallest local political jurisdiction possible (except when funds of nonlocal governments can be used without compromising independence and uniqueness). And this is all for the use of those who are able and willing, provided they are taxpayers of that same local jurisdiction.

Three key limiting factors of this paradigm are:

Excessive focus by librarianship on (1) the organization of knowledge and physical units; (2) acquisition for ownership in case an item may be needed; and (3) service *availability*

The institutional emphasis of public libraries on *local*—local ownership, local funding and local use

The general conceptual model for the respective roles of local, state, and federal government in the funding of public library services

Excessive Professional Focus

A primary focus of librarianship as a profession is on *organization.* Organization is viewed as an intrinsic good. The more organization (subject headings, categories, pigeonholes, structure, etc.) there is, the better things are. Organizing everything—knowledge, physical units (such as books), statistics, and associations—down to the smallest elements possible seems to be a professional obsession. This proclivity goes far beyond legitimate utilitarian worth. It appears to be an end in itself, rather than as a means to service delivery. Organizing things seems to have become librarianship's world view.

Acquisition for ownership is another primary professional focus that increasingly is excessive and outmoded. Public librarians legitimately have acquired collections for their communities' use. However, collection size has come inappropriately to be seen as being largely synonymous with effectiveness in service delivery.

Now public librarians are limiting the effectiveness of their institutions by fostering an inordinate drive for "acquisition" that goes far beyond collection growth. Books, tapes, buildings, cities, and counties are acquired to be "owned" by the library system. The size of the collection and the number and capacity of buildings are assumed to be measures of library greatness. Ownership has become an inordinately important and increasingly limited self-imposed standard of library and librarian success.

The equation of *service availability* with *service delivery* is another very limiting concept in public librarianship. This problem is linked with the obsession of acquisition. Making library services *available* to the public is essential; but it is only a very important *means* to the end of service *delivery*. Offering accessibility by placing a library in a community is not the same as placing a book in users' hands.

Organizing a library according to a scheme of knowledge and buying a collection of materials and piacing them in a community library are important activities that should be seen as one set of means toward service delivery. These strategies should not be viewed as the only ones available to libraries. They certainly should not be seen as ends for the service delivery chain.

Inappropriate Local Institutional Emphases

Another major confining public library concept is that "local is good." Local sufficiency, use by local constituents (taxpayers), a local tax base, local ownership, and control by local government—all are dearly held concepts for public libraries. The concept of local ownership of collections and buildings is a fundamental tenet in public-libraryland. This concept is tightly related to the symbol of size as a measure of success. This paradigm reinforces the need for ownership by acquisition of physical units for the collection. Achieving local ownership of another 1,000 or 10,000 or 100,000 volumes is viewed as having a more successful library.

Local funding is also a highly valued fundamental good in most public library circles. Local taxes are synonymous with local government and local administrative control. Local control is the goal of most public library administrators. Local government is a goal heartily preferred by most citizens.

A natural corollary to the concepts of local ownership of collections and local funding is that "the local library is for local taxpayers." With logic, outsiders are excluded because they have not contributed to the local tax supporting the local library. Although nonresident fees provide a method for joining the local tax base, this choice for individual nonresidents does not provide a public library as an effective substitute for economies of scale possible with the larger market base offered by serving multiple jurisdictions.

This local world view perpetuates public library organization based upon the smallest political jurisdiction possible. It perpetuates public library service limited to taxpayers of those jurisdiction. It also perpetuates creation of the largest local libraries possible within the smallest political jurisdiction possible. Further, this local world view wastes opportunities for more effective use of resources through the development of shared systems.

INEFFECTIVE PARADIGM ABOUT GOVERNMENT FUNDING ROLES

The world view that local is good sets the stage for most public library funding relationships. The principle held dear by most public library administrators and policymakers is that both the administrative control and funding for public library services should reside in the same location. The preferred location for control of public library policy, priorities, and administration has been as local as is practical. Therefore, the primary funding body for most public libraries is local government.

State government usually is seen as a supplementary funding provider. States generally have assumed a role that is primarily as provider of standards for local libraries in matters of finance, facilities, and personnel. This is accomplished through audits, building standards, and certification of librarians.

Given the prevailing fundamental assumption that public libraries are and should be a local service locally controlled and funded, it is not surprising that the federal government's role in public library finance has been even more limited than that of the states. The federal government largely has limited its role to providing ancillary funding and gathering statistics. Needless to say, the federal government has underplayed its potential in developing public library services.

It would be inaccurate to state that the federal government has had no positive impact on public library services. However, it would be appropriate to state that, generally, the federal government has provided relatively little funding for public library services, and even less stable ongoing funding. The federal government has focused its efforts on providing grant funds for outreach services and facilities construction. Neither arena has received the consistent and greater funding attention needed. Often, the monies available through federal grants, especially for services, have been too little for the paperwork involved. The other historical (and relatively passive) federal role has been that of collecting statistics. Unfortunately, these generally are already outdated when published.

INEFFICIENT PARADIGMS

The problem with the values and viewpoints we hold related to public libraries is that they produce a paradigm that is ineffective in solving old, persistent problems. More important, the current paradigm increasingly will inhibit solving future problems and taking advantage of new opportunities. The currently held world view contains models that will allow libraries and librarians to continue along the paths they now know. However, that world view will not enable public libraries to obtain greater resources and attract larger numbers of users. More important, that world view will not allow public libraries to evolve successfully. As the environment shifts and change compounds change, public library service, as we now know it, not only will continue to be inaccessible to some and inconvenient to many, but it also will become irrelevant to most people.

A paradigm, according to Joel A. Barker (1989, p. 14), "is a set of rules and regulations that: (1) defines boundaries; and, (2) tells you what to do to be successful within those boundaries. (Success is measured by the problems you solve using these rules and regulations.)" Those involved in making and influencing policy about public library service will need to develop a different paradigm if they are to act responsibly, not to mention effectively, in their roles.

Public library service policymakers and administrators need to develop a new set of rules and regulations, values and viewpoints, and a world view for successfully dealing with increasingly difficult trends and issues. These new and old persistent unsolved problems include the generally reduced availability of local funding; the decreasing relative financial importance of individual local units of government; widespread electronic publishing; an information pricing structure based on use not ownership; increasing access to information through telecommunications; growing pluralism in the nation's culture; and larger numbers of functionally illiterate adults.

Although all of these trends have been present for years, if not decades, their size and rate of change are having an ever-increasing impact on librarianship as a profession, on public libraries as institutions, and on their product, public library service. The profession and the institution (the two means toward the end) must find new ways of seeing and dealing with the changing environment in which they act for the delivery of public library service. The profession and the institution must create new relationships and use different methods if they are to be effective in meeting the needs of public library service. In fact, if the public librarianship and public libraries are to survive long enough to become relevant to a majority of the nation's population, both will need to adapt and change themselves.

A NECESSARY PARADIGM SHIFT

Identifying and making the necessary changes will not be an easy effort. There are no specific and unalterable formulas for creating and delivering effective public library services. Public library service is not a mass-produced product. Public libraries are not factories. Librarianship is not a science.

However, there are lessons to be learned from Thomas Kuhn's writings (1970, pp. 182–187). Librarianship, as practiced in public library service, will need to develop a disciplinary matrix for its use in considering how to be effective in future decades. Included should be the equivalent of Kuhn's "symbolic generalizations," those expressions used without question or protest; shared beliefs to which librarianship is committed; widely shared values within the library community; and "exemplars" (or shared examples) for concrete solutions of problems. This new disciplinary matrix will need to reexamine many of the premises underlying, as well as most of the methods now used for establishing, public library institutions and providing public library services.

It is time for a major paradigm shift. The cost efficiency of our current paradigms for public library service is too low. (See Barker, pp. 78–89 for a discussion of paradigm cost efficiency.) A new model is required, if there is to be efficient problem solving for public library service. A new model is necessary soon, if there is to be an effective future for public library service.

Barker recounts (pp. 59–60) the development of the digital watch. Swiss manufacturers, who had perfected analog watchmaking, were among those who failed to see the importance of the digital watch concept when it was first exhibited at a trade show. However, Japanese industry and the U.S. firm of Texas Instruments did perceive the nature of the coming revolution and took appropriate action. The Swiss manufacturers finally entered the market as a catch-up player.

Barker also reviews (pp. 90–96) the story of IBM, the Goliath of computer manufacturers, and Apple, who played David in his analogy. IBM had achieved immense success through a set of fundamental rules used in its business. These rules included manufacturing its own microprocessors, writing its own software, and selling its own products. Apple created a revolution in manufacturing personal computers and became a major competitor to IBM by disregarding the "rules." Apple could not afford to manufacture its own microprocessors so it contracted for their production. Apple did not have the staff to write the needed software, so that too was purchased. Apple had no sales force, so it sold its products through other retailers.

IBM then used another of its fundamental rules (always maintain a fair share of the market), scrapped its three other fundamental rules, and adopted Apple's rules. Apple not only created a new product, it created a new paradigm for the computer manufacturing business.

There must be a shift in the paradigm used by public library service because the old rules are no longer successful in solving continuing persistent problems. Moreover, public libraries and librarians are operating in a world where other organizations and disciplines are making new rules affecting public library service.

The old persistent major problems include inadequate funding

41

from all sources; the shortage of new professional librarians; too little research about users, nonusers, and service competency; too little development of new models for service delivery; and an absence of planning for future public library service. New rules from the public library community are required if there are to be new effective solutions rather than old, tired, ineffective solutions. New rules are being handed out with increasing frequency by others.

The pricing structure for information has changed and continues to change rapidly. Information costs are now priced by the hit, by the minute, and by the number of users. The days of purchasing a physical unit might not yet be numbered, but a new pricing age is approaching swiftly. Public libraries have not yet adjusted to and are ill-prepared to adapt to this pricing revolution.

The problem of the physical unit that contains needed information but is in circulation is itself quickly becoming an irrelevant concept. When electronic information is "in play," it is not the same as when a physical volume is "in use" or "in circulation." Electronically formatted information, practically speaking, is always available, and accessible almost simultaneously at multiple locations with virtually no waiting. This radical shift alters the landscape of access. Service availability to walk-in users is no longer (if it ever was) a sufficient success measure for access to public library service.

Public library service has not even begun to make effective use of the new electronic information capabilities. In fact, we continue to make old use of new technology. Most public libraries offering access to electronic materials do so by acquiring multiple hard copies on compact digital disks. Often, these are used like reference books, sequentially at work stations after being manually inserted into the disk drives. Such use is almost as ludicrous as attempting to play a music compact disc on a phonograph record player.

REVISING THE PUBLIC LIBRARY PARADIGM

Public libraries are designed for walk-in use at a time when walk-in service is increasingly not good enough. Public libraries maintain extensive inventories *just in case* they are needed, rather than providing access on time *when* it is needed. Such libraries are only organized for knowledge when users are searching for solutions to problems.

Public libraries are funded and controlled by the smallest political jurisdiction possible at the same time that highly mobile populations are sprawled over many political boundaries. Public libraries seek local (and preferably unique) solutions to generic public library service problems.

Public librarians and public library policymakers must play a new game still using an old set of rules. New sets of rules are required for a professional focus, for institutional emphases, and for the roles of government in public library service.

New Professional Focus

Professionals need to recognize that the primary business of libraries is the transfer of ideas and information. Organizing information and making it available are important activities but they do not constitute service delivery. People use libraries to obtain ideas and information in various packages *as a means* toward solving problems, learning how to solve problems, and for sheer pleasure. It is important that we focus more on service delivery, the end result of organizing and creating service availability.

New Institutional Emphases

Public library service needs to be unbundled. It is no longer necessary, or even always desirable, to place in the same location a freestanding building, books, and staff. Service accessibility can be creatively and cost-effectively provided through new and different sites, with ITM's (information transfer machines) backed up by live human beings who can communicate clearly with users. Staff in library boutiques located in social service agencies, office buildings, and shopping malls can provide on-target, on-time service using electronic support systems.

Planning, evaluating, and service development experiments need to be undertaken on a large-scale multiple site basis, not just in individual, isolated single-library system situations. System-sharing (and not just cooperative acquisition and document location identification protocols) needs to be developed for cost efficient on-time service delivery on metropolitan, statewide, and national bases.

New Government Roles Partnership

There need to be new partnerships among local, state, and federal governments in the functional and funding roles that they provide in public library service. The forging of new partnerships is essential because of the vast changes in society since the inception of public libraries. These vast changes have affected not only the populations to be served, but also the profession and institutions designed to do the serving.

New Functional Relationship

Local government should be primarily responsible for ensuring the responsiveness of public library service to specific community needs. The setting of policies and priorities, the managing of the library system, and delivering service should be the responsibility of local government.

State government should be predominately responsible for the functions of oversight and coordination of public library services. Planning for shared systems and service delivery improvements, ensuring fiscal and staff competence, and confirming that service delivery levels meet or exceed minimum standards throughout the state are important active functional roles for state government.

The federal government should be actively engaged in research, development, and standards for public library service. This major activist federal role should include both leadership and funding dimensions. Such a research function would provide for the collection of needed documentation about service effectiveness and service needs. The broader national perspective and amount of funds that could be provided offer a unique opportunity for the comparison of various types of delivery methods and circumstances, as well as information about the absolute effectiveness of existing and demonstration programs. Research is needed about the people using public library services, and how, when, and how much they use public library services. Further, information is needed about the people who do not use public library services and why they don't.

The federal government's developmental role should encompass the formation and demonstration of service delivery models. Experimentation with multitype library delivery systems, services to rural residents, and many other areas need funding and evaluation. The usefulness and viability of entrepreneurial libraries should be explored to determine if they can provide cost-efficient, delivery-effective services shared on a cost-recovery basis through contracts with other libraries.

In the area of technical development, the federal role would be to assist the advancement of technical standards and the design and configuration of hardware and software for shared electronic systems for information resources and networks. The federal role could be

44

instrumental in the implementation of telecommunication systems for public library services.

New Funding Relationship

The new partnership for governmental funding of public library services would shift the local, state, and federal roles with the federal government taking on a larger and a more direct role. The federal role would provide significantly for the research, developmental, and technical assistance projects already discussed. In addition to these direct, contract, and grant activities, the federal role would take on a new philosophical dimension of direct per capita funding to public library systems for *compensatory* services.

Compensatory funding for public library services would be an extension of similar federal funding for public education needs at the local level. This approach uses a funding formula that provides additional monies for augmented services directed to the disadvantaged. These could include all who are unable to use public library services due to illiteracy, insufficient learning skills and/or language proficiency; geography; physical abilities; and/or income level.

State governments would be responsible for funding public library services throughout each state at a moderate level. This level of funding would be sufficient to provide highly adequate service in all geographical areas based on individual state standards.

Local funding would still be necessary. However, rather than being the primary funding source as is now the case for most public libraries, local funding would concentrate on providing for *special local option* services and augmenting the service levels available through state government funding. This decision-making about meeting special local needs also would include local allocation of federal aid granted directly to public libraries.

Thus, state and federal funds would become more important in the financing of public library services throughout the nation. The states would guarantee an adequate level of service for all residents and communities, with the concurrent development of coordinated, cost-effective shared systems. Responsiveness to local needs would continue to be the responsibility of local jurisdictions.

CREATING THE NEW PARADIGM

The proposed greatly enhanced funding role of the federal government and its certain increased interest in the effective use of its monies would add impetus for a more active leadership and development role. This role likely would be as great in developing an effective future for public libraries as that of the role of direct per capita grants to local library systems.

This proposed very significant change in the federal funding role is not likely to occur without many of the other conceptual changes already discussed. A fundamental shift such as this requires a realignment of many factors and factions. Additionally, this and other changes advanced here obviously would require modifications and a number of years for their acceptance and implementation.

It is the change in the mindset, the world view, about public library service that is the most urgent and critical need. This paradigm shift is the essential key to needed change. Without a reassessment and reconfiguration of old values and viewpoints, few other significant changes can or will occur in public library service. A new mental landscape is required for an effective public library future. Such a future is possible *if* we change the rules on how we think about library services and resources. If we create a new mental landscape for the new environment in which public libraries and their users will exist, then we can solve many of the old, persistent problems. We will be able to resolve many of the "too littles"—too little money, too few professionals, too little useful research, too little effective development projects, and too little planning for future services. The resolution of these problems might not be found in just more money, but in doing things and using resources differently.

New paradigms about effectiveness are required. We must shift the professional focus from *organization* to *transfer*. Public libraries as institutions need to focus on *solutions* rather than on *acquisitions*. They must unbundle books, buildings, and bodies from their traditional clusters and rooted locations for greater flexibility, efficiency, and responsiveness. Government roles need to shift, with the federal role becoming greatly enhanced in the areas of leadership, research, service development, and direct funding of public library services.

The key strategy to such changes, indeed to any effective response in the new public library service environment, is for each person involved in public library service delivery to change the rules. Changing the ways we think about public library service is necessary. Only then can we become better able to solve the persistent old problems and the new emerging problems that are barriers to an effective future for public library service.

All the changes proposed require the creation and use of a different mental framework that encompasses the new realities facing public library policymakers, public library service providers, and public library users.

REFERENCES

Barker, Joel A. *Discovering the Future: The Business of Paradigms.* 3rd ed. St. Paul, MN: ILI Press, 1989.

Covey, Stephen R. *The Seven Habits of Highly Effective People: Restoring the Character Ethic.* New York: Simon & Schuster, 1989.

Kuhn, Thomas S. *The Structure of Scientific Revolutions.* 2d ed., enl. Vol. 2, no. 2 of *Foundations of the Unity of Science, International Encyclopedia of Unified Science.* Chicago: University of Chicago Press, 1970.

PART 2

State Funding of Academic and Public Libraries

State Aid to Libraries: A National Perspective

Barratt Wilkins
State Librarian
State Library of Florida
Tallahassee, Florida

Over the years, I have researched and written many papers. They were written by a trained historian, who became a librarian with an avocation for history, and who is now a middle-aged, somewhat historically curious senior government manager. It never ceases to amaze me that despite the great changes we have seen in our lifetimes and those that have been witnessed over the last 150 years, much remains the same—packaged differently perhaps, but still the same.

My topic here is the scintillating and provocative one of "State Aid to Libraries: A National Perspective." The subject of state aid to libraries has occupied my tenure as state librarian as few other topics have. Indeed, while the love of money may be the root of all evil, money itself is also the root of considerable progress.

I discuss three separate developments that largely emerged in the nineteenth century and how they came together to become the foundation of the modern concept of state aid. That historical overview is followed by a discussion of state aid as we see it today and the emergence of some four levels of support: the establishment of shares of support in our federalist system; what characterizes various state aid programs; a few suggestions of success; and this "poor lights" vision of the future.

The first of the historical developments was the emergence of state libraries early in the nineteenth century. Between 1816 and 1819,

Illinois, New Hampshire, New York, Ohio, and Pennsylvania established state libraries, primarily for the use of their legislatures. However, the 1818 act creating the New York State Library declared its objective was to found "a public library for the use of government and of the people of the state." By the time of the great landmark survey of public libraries in 1876, each one of the forty-four states and territories had established a state library. It was not until the 1890s that a few of these state libraries and state library commissions gained authorization for a role in public library development and the extension of public library services.

The second historical development was the emergence of public libraries in the mid-nineteenth century from the roots of privately funded societal and association libraries to the free public libraries supported in whole or in part by local government funding. State laws providing for creation of free public libraries since the mid-nineteenth century have been permissive in nature—not mandatory. Thus, states have permitted local enthusiasm to take the initiative to establish and extend public libraries. While public libraries were seen in the nineteenth century to be centers of lifelong learning, they have always been viewed as adjuncts to public education; not integral facets.

And, of course, the third important development in the nineteenth century was the establishment of public education on a mandated and compulsory level. To this movement, *states* have supported and funded compulsory and consolidated public education at a ratio above the 50 percent level.

By the early 1900s, these three developments began to interact with one another to form the foundation of the concept of state aid to public libraries. In 1875, Rhode Island became the first state to authorize its board of education to grant sums of money to existing public libraries. In 1890 and 1891, Massachusetts and New Hampshire established library commissions to make grants of money to public libraries. By the early 1900s, a number of states had followed this pattern, but many observers at that time felt the grants were so small as to have very little significance.

I think those early patterns were more significant than early writers on library development and the public library may have wanted to believe. Those patterns, with some exceptions, mark the modern view of public libraries:

1. The public library is largely a local institution supported largely by local tax dollars
2. Whereas state governments mandated systems of public

education and supported education at above the 50 percent level through state taxation, states *did not* mandate public libraries and did not, for the most part, support public libraries generously from state taxation

3. States have authorized state library agencies to encourage public library establishment, extension, and development and have provided a system of state grants-in-aid to local libraries

Modern state aid programs began in the 1930s with the goals of:

- assisting impoverished local governments in meeting library resource needs
- encouraging larger units of service, where the tax burden could be more economically distributed. (The county and regional library concept encouraged by California State Librarian James Gillis in the first twenty years of this century began this movement toward larger units of service.)
- equalizing library service, particularly in states with a wide disparity between the rich and the poor

Ohio established the first modern state aid program in 1935.

Dean F. William Summers, Florida State University, the School of Library and Information Studies, suggested earlier in some unpublished remarks drawn from experienced observation that a few types of state aid had emerged where:

1. States such as Hawaii and West Virginia substantially support public library service
2. States such as Illinois and New York support larger systems whose boundaries have been established at the state level
3. States such as California, Florida, and South Carolina assist in aiding libraries with minimal state regulation
4. States such as Massachusetts and some of the other New England states provide aid to any library that has been legally established

As far as I have been able to determine, there is no empirically validated formula for establishing shares of support for public library service at the federal, state, and local levels. In a 1973–1974 report to the National Commission on Libraries and Information Science, by Government Studies and Systems, it was recommended that the proportions of support for public library service be 20 percent federal, 50 percent state, and 30 percent local. In many states, the pattern has been more like 15 percent from federal, state, and other sources, and 85 percent from local sources. Indeed, a report of public library income in the United States, published by the University of Illinois, as expressed by the percentage of states in each pattern, showed:

60% local special property taxes
28% local general revenue
6% local taxes (i.e., percent of gas/cigarette/road taxes)
4% state aid (Hawaii, West Virginia)
2% state income tax (Ohio)

In the last national survey of state aid to libraries, published in 1984 and compiled and edited by Nancy Bolt, now state librarian of Colorado, it detailed the types of distribution formulas used by states in allocating aid dollars.

23 states distributed on per capita formula (e.g., Georgia, Illinois, Missouri)

13 states had an equalization formula (e.g., Illinois, Florida, Maryland)

11 states provided base grants for public library service (e.g., Alaska, Connecticut, Indiana, Minnesota, Nebraska)

6 states provided discretionary grants in aid (e.g., Arizona, Arkansas, Kansas, Nevada)

4 states had area aid (e.g., Minnesota, Idaho)

4 states provided aid in terms of reimbursements (e.g., Michigan, New Mexico, New York)

Bolt also provided an overview of eligibility requirements for libraries to receive state aid, with the most frequently cited being the specification of legal establishment (27 states), maintenance of effort at the local level (25 states), and the requirement that certain written documents be submitted (23 states). These written documents might include proof that the librarian graduated from an ALA-accredited program, the library's personnel plan for classification and pay, and the library's long-range plan. Other eligibility requirements cited less frequently were:

19 trained personnel
18 minimum local budget

17   hours of public access
14   percentage or amount of local tax support
11   membership in networks, cooperatives, systems
10   material to be shared with other libraries, and several others

Now let us examine the efforts of the states to finance state aid to library programs. These efforts are characterized in per capita figures and were reported in the *1990 State Library Agencies Financial Survey*, prepared by the Council of State Governments for the Chief Officers of State Library Agencies. Based on the FY 1990 appropriations for state aid to libraries, the following generalizations may be drawn:

- Highest per capita state aid programs are in northern states, with the exception of Georgia
- Florida falls in the moderate support category as 17th in per capita
- The minimal support category of from 50¢ to just under $1 per capita was largely southern and western states
- The poorest support states are those with 11¢ per capita or less; they are mainly western states

STATE AIDE, FY 1990 APPROPRIATIONS

1.	Georgia	5.66
2.	Maryland	4.21
3.	New York	4.01
4.	Rhode Island	3.51
5.	West Virginia	3.06
6.	Illinois	2.83
7.	Massachusetts	2.90
8.	Pennsylvania	2.50
9.	Wisconsin	2.12
10.	New Jersey	2.11
17.	Florida	1.32
20.	Mississippi	1.16
21.	Alabama	1.09
22.	South Carolina	.94
23.	Colorado	.88

24.	Arkansas	.80
25.	Iowa	.72
25.	Connecticut	.72
27.	North Dakota	.69
28.	Montana	.67
29.	Kansas	.64
30.	Oklahoma	.53
41.	New Hamp-shire	.11
42.	New Mexico	.10
43.	Nevada	.07
44.	Wyoming	.02
45.	Louisiana	.00

It is interesting to note that those states with the highest per capita state support, and that first established state libraries, first established compulsory education, first established state aid to libraries laws, and first passed permissive public library establishment laws, have, with some exceptions, had among the best supported public libraries in the nation. These states are Maryland, New York, Rhode Island, West Virginia, Illinois, Massachusetts, Pennsylvania, Wisconsin, and New Jersey. Leading all of the states in state aid support per capita is Georgia. But the anomaly of Georgia is that it is the home state of Henry W. Grady, that great force for the "New South," a movement characterized by economic strength and forward attitudes.

Perhaps I should stop here and not offer any thoughts on the future, but I cannot resist the temptation.

As far as federal aid to libraries is concerned, I think it is a terribly endangered species. I am not suggesting that we stop fighting for such aid, but that we not be surprised if it is discontinued in the next few years. My reasons are these: an administration with a 90 percent approval rating (in the spring of 1991) that has recommended steep cuts in federal aid to libraries; a staggering national debit of unprecedented proportions, which in time can only lead to national economic depression; the attitude of the majority of taxpayers who are against increased taxes regardless of the socioeconomic consequences; and the failure of a sense of community and the common good among Americans.

State aid to libraries may be an endangered species itself in five to ten years. Again, we should not stop fighting for these resources, but we must recognize economic realities. My reasons for this belief are the shift of federal programs to states with fewer resources to provide the former national programs, thus cutting what are viewed as nonessential services; the fact that most state government are prohibited from debt financing and are confined to balanced budgets; the overwhelming fear of legislatures to tax; and the attitude of a majority of taxpayers, who are against increased taxes regardless of the consequences. If you could eavesdrop on my conversations with colleagues across the country, you, too, would be concerned. There are not many states that have remained untouched.

- California has a $10 billion deficit; state aid to libraries has been cut by 50 percent
- Vermont's state library agency has been reduced by 24 percent
- Double digit percentage cuts have been taken in Rhode Island, Massachusetts, Tennessee, Florida, Minnesota, Virginia, New York, New Jersey, and other states

Perhaps state libraries will return to their original missions to serve the information needs of state government and its agencies. And I do not see this trend stopping soon.

So, what about local funding? This is perhaps the salvation of the public library as an American institution. The closer the service is to the people that it serves, the more likelihood for community support. And it will put increased pressure on public library directors and friends and trustee organizations to make this service more attractive and viable.

Recently I commented to one state representative that I had never seen a time when all government financing had become "soft and fluid." This description used to be applied only to federal funds. It is quickly becoming apparent that soft and fluid applies to all levels of government financing.

Perhaps the best I can advise is that each of us must look for more doors in the walls against which we are living. I wish you good fortune in finding those doors!

State Funding for Academic Libraries

Ralph E. Russell
University Librarian
Georgia State University, Pullen Library
Atlanta, Georgia

The scope of this paper includes funding for all college and university libraries in the 1990s—whether public or private. What is now needed for academic libraries are resources of various kinds, but the availability of those resources is severely limited in the short term and the competition for them is keen, indeed. Our efforts to garner necessary funding for libraries ought to be rational, informed, mission-driven, and with a reasonable prospect for success. A witty friend, recently appointed acting president at Georgia State, noted at his initial meeting with the faculty that he planned to eschew the management philosophy stated in his favorite bumper sticker: "Until morale improves, the flogging will continue!" Things are *not* that bad! Before reviewing what is needed and feasible in funding from state governments, it is appropriate to examine the present status and near-term predictions for higher education and its libraries and the economic landscape among the states.

First, the present academic library environment: We're between a rock and a hard place. Caught between the rock of static or—worse yet—actually declining budgets and the hard place of relentlessly rising costs for serial subscriptions and books, we're struggling to keep the doors open. As noted by Okerson and Stubbs (1991): "The pattern of scholarly journal prices increasing two and three times as rapidly as the Consumer Price Index in the 1980s persists and will intensify in the early 1990s" (p. 36).*

Academic libraries are cancelling journal subscriptions and buying fewer monographs. The net result is less access to information for library users. This litany of woes is one you know. With diminishing buying power, more and more of us are watching collections become outdated. We're borrowing more books from one another. But resource sharing means *somebody* has to own a document and be willing to lend it. Therein lies our mandate for cooperative collection development and cooperation generally. Given our inadequate budgets, it will certainly be a renewed priority for the 1990s.

Because of the drain on resources to purchase materials, staff services are suffering. A university administrator recently called for less intermediation—he meant less reference service. Less staff assistance may be advocated, ironically, at precisely the time when our users need more help finding information from diverse sources, formats, and delivery systems. All too frequently, budget cutbacks mean staff layoffs or elimination of positions. Our automated systems may be user friendly, but the pace at our service desks has increased.

Our physical facilities are overflowing and beginning to show the strain of inadequate maintenance and housekeeping budgets. The comfort and safety of our users, and their reasonable access to information and materials, are imperiled in many instances. Space for collections is a continuing dilemma. Funds planned for preservation of our collections are drastically diminished or eliminated altogether. If the choice is between new materials and preserving older materials, most of us will opt for the new.

The colleges and universities where we exist are macrocosms of our fiscal woes. Although the tenured faculty remains intact in most instances, cost reductions, furloughs, staff rosters downsized, tuition increases, drastically diminished (or eliminated) travel and supply budgets, programs dropped, freezes on new hires—all are part of current coping with the economic times.

Carolyn Mooney (1991) summed it up: "Across the nation, elite universities and small colleges alike are cutting their budgets and scaling back their operations to deal with current and anticipated financial problems" (p. Al).

It is *not* business as usual. As we scramble to keep our doors open and our basic functions intact, it is a time for reviewing mission statements and institutional priorities . . . and some hard choices.

And the economies of our states? Dismal! In general terms, most

---

* The references in this chapter can be found in the Bibliography on pp. 109.

of them are in fiscal crisis. At least thirty-seven states are facing deficits unless they raise taxes, cut spending, or employ some combination of the two (Blumenstyle 1991, p. 1). The mood of taxpayers is strongly opposed to raising taxes. In referring to recent referenda on library bond issues, Nolan T. Yelich, Virginia Deputy State Librarian, said: "Voters suggested that the general public is not interested in raising taxes or authorizing any activity at the local and state level that would further reduce levels of personal income even at the expense of reductions and/or eliminations of vital public services including those provided by libraries" ("Special LJ Roundup," 1991, p. 36).

Most states are addressing the problem by cutting spending; sometimes a combination of spending cuts and increased taxes is employed. For the purpose of this discussion, we can summarize and say that it is a new day in the competition for state funding. It is a tougher day. Given the limited state resources and the competition for them, libraries must demonstrate both compelling need for additional resources and evident links between their purpose and society's goals.

So, welcome to the 1990s . . . to that awful place between the rock and the hard place. The present reality is gloomy. Predictions of when the economy will improve vary. It seems more guesswork than science. Some economists predict at least eighteen more months before we experience substantial improvement. And although the economic pendulum *will* swing back to more prosperous times, we may witness some fundamental changes in library funding and our relationships with users. Inevitably, we will have choices!

And we *do* have the option to seek increased state funding for our academic libraries. The rationale for state support for academic libraries, what a state-funded library network ought to provide, and two models of such networks follow.

RATIONALE FOR STATE SUPPORT

I am assuming that state support for academic libraries most appropriately would be channeled through a library cooperative or network. In my view it is more likely that a network of libraries could better persuade a state legislative body to fund its collaborative efforts than a single institution could. The political influence of librarians and library supporters united throughout a state would be a powerful source to garner funding. In making tough dollar allocation decisions, statewide educational benefit is more compelling to a legislator as rationale for funding than benefit accruing to a much smaller subset of that population.

First, libraries working together, sharing resources, offer maximum use of a body of materials, services, and assets. Effective resource sharing means that a citizen anywhere in the state has access to information and material beyond the borders of his/her county or region. This is of major concern to elected government officials who wish to have a positive impact on the lives of constituents. And having just reviewed the economy of our states generally, I believe that a priority for state government ought to be the squeezing of maximum value from each dollar appropriated for education. Library resource sharing, because it maximizes benefit for each expenditure, ought to appeal to state legislatures and officials.

Second, state support for a library network for resource sharing is relevant and appropriate because enhanced information access addresses, in a tangible way, the development of an informed citizenry. It is pivotal to our form of government. Thomas Jefferson said it best and most succinctly in 1816: "If a nation expects to be ignorant and free, in a state of civilization, it expects what never was and never will be."

To wield the power of the ballot effectively, our citizens must be informed and their vision must extend beyond the confines of Hahira, Georgia, or Samoset, Florida. The Bible says, and I paraphrase, "You shall know the truth and the truth shall make you free." But first one must know the truth!

Third, providing access to information resources is important for economic development. Information does play a critical role in economic development. We are concerned that we compete effectively in that international marketplace. As David Osborne (1990) says, we have witnessed the death of the industrial economy and the birth of a new economy—one that is information dependent. Because we cannot compete with low-cost, unskilled labor in the manufacturing marketplace, we must compete on innovation, advanced technologies, and knowledge-intensive products and services. In Osborne's words: "Our future, in short, depends upon our ability to innovate and our ability to use our minds, which means our most valuable resources are no longer things such as raw materials and cheap labor. Our most valuable resources are people who can innovate and the information they need to do so" (p. 57).

Fourth, our collaboration assures maximum benefit for dollars spent. Sharing library resources may eliminate some redundancy with some cost savings and greatly expand the array of information available to our users. Please note that cost savings is not at the top of my list; I would never begin my pitch for a state-supported library network by touting its money-saving characteristics! With communication and coordination among librarians, cooperative collection development can expand the array of information available to users without unnecessary duplicated materials. The important point is that each new library collection added to a library network means new information for users. In a study of twenty-one of the twenty-two academic libraries participating in the Illinois Library Computer System in the early 1980s, Potter (1986) found that as machine-readable bibliographic holdings files for each library collection were added to the central database, "a high percentage of titles, 69.46 percent, occurred only once in the network and that a percentage of the collection of each library, ranging from 6.1 percent to 68.4 percent, was unique to that library" (p. 119).

It is evident that library collections are not the same collection of books and journals duplicated from site to site.

Last, all of these consequences of better libraries and enhanced access to information are quality-of-life considerations. Libraries are a critical component in the array of cultural/educational/recreational offerings a community provides for its citizens.

LIBRARY NETWORK

What ought a statewide network of libraries offer its members and ultimately, all library users? I've thought about my own institution and what we must have to support and encourage resource sharing. Targeted grants to encourage interlibrary lending, to convert paper catalog records into machine readable form, and to purchase materials in specific subject areas—all speak to current needs where I work.

Here are some things I would want the library network (if we had one) in my state to encourage:

1. Resource sharing
   a. Telecommunications network
   b. Bibliographic database of collections owned, with holdings indicated
   c. Protocols for borrowing
   d. Rapid document delivery–user initiated ILL
   e. External databases
   f. Shared full text

2. Cooperative collection development
   a. Collection assessment so that we can build on collection strengths
   b. Collecting responsibilities
   c. Stimulus money for targeted collection building
3. Training/staff development
4. Storage facility for infrequently used library materials

This laundry list represents only what I want from a state-funded library network. But the entire list is feasible and represents what, in my view, many academic libraries need.

State funding *can* make a difference as a stimulus for collaborative activities and for investing in collections that clearly are for the good of all. Even though he has been enormously successful in fostering library cooperation, the state librarian of Florida, with tongue in cheek, has called library cooperation an unnatural act! At times, in building cooperative relationships and structure, it seems so. The decision makers I know in higher education are not necessarily persuaded to commit resources because it is a "good thing to do." How it will make *us* more effective as an institution seems to be the key question. Will *we* benefit? Precisely *what* and *how* will be benefit? State funding along the lines I've outlined would be a strong stimulus for participation from any institution . . . "unnatural" though it may be.

CURRENT MODELS

For our discussion, I have chosen two statewide models to describe. The first is a network of academic libraries within a higher education coordinating body; the second is a multitype library network operated within a state library.

The Network of Alabama Academic Libraries was established in 1984 "to identify ways in which the state's academic libraries might better cooperate and to provide a mechanism for resource sharing activities" (Medina 1987, p. 41).

NAAL was a response to a study that found that "Alabama's libraries were lagging far behind their regional peers in every aspect of measurement: physical plant, journal collections, book holdings, and size of staff" (Medina 1987, p. 44). What have they wrought in the past seven years? Much!

- They've just completed an on-line bibliographic database of over seven million records with holdings for their twenty general members and six cooperative members. A retrospective conversion effort was strongly stimulated by state funds.

- In its first year, the network operated on members' contributions. But ever since, they have been funded at the level of $500,000 per year or more.
- They have used collection assessment techniques to identify collection levels for support of graduate study and research.
- Funds are budgeted to reimburse libraries that are net lenders to other consortium members.
- Funds are provided to purchase collections in assigned subject areas of existing strength for all members.

1988/89	1989/90	1990/91	TOTAL 1985–1991
$704,757	$671,075	$667,907	$2,480,739

- Continuing education and training are part of the consortium program, particularly in the training for the use of technology in libraries.
- Communication among academic librarians at all levels is high.

Their members are enthusiastic about the results of their collaboration and the investment made by their state. The legislature must be satisfied because it continues to fund the library network with annual increases. Dr. Medina (1991), Executive Director of NAAL, says:

> State funding for NAAL has also purchased a valuable but intangible asset: a cooperative spirit. While libraries in many states discuss the benefits of cooperation, few have engaged in as many productive cooperative programs as Alabama's academic libraries. With very small funding levels, NAAL members have fully converted bibliographic records for print materials into OCLC, reduced average document delivery times from nine to five days, improved the quality of collections supporting graduate education and strengthened the abilities of library staff to provide meaningful library services. (letter)

The second type of network is Illinet, a multitype, statewide network based in Illinois and part of the Illinois State Library. It began in 1965 under state legislation and has gone through several stages of evolution to reach its present membership of more than 2,000 libraries of all types. Its legitimacy and purpose are spelled out in the Illinois Library Law, which states:

> the function of the State Library is to promote and develop a cooperative library network operating regionally or statewide for providing effective coordination of the library resources of public, academic, school, and special libraries, and to promote and develop information centers for improved supplemental library services for special library clientele served by each type of library or center. (LaCroix 1987, p. 19)

Illinet has five major program emphases:

1. Document delivery. Requests are transmitted using OCLC, TWX, and library automated circulation systems. Libraries use established protocols in determining from whom to request materials. Because of the richness of Illinois library collections, most requests can be filled within the state. Since 1980 there has been a statewide truck delivery service. That is supplemented now by UPS, commercial buses, and the U.S. Postal Service, and telefacsimile transmission is increasingly used for document delivery.

2. OCLC and Bibliographic Access/Illinet Online. As an OCLC network, Illinet provides staff support, training programs, contract administration, and accounting for OCLC charges. The general members pay only OCLC direct costs. Illinet members are provided with training, publications for staying current, and consulting services. Since 1981, the sharing of automated library systems and online catalogs has been encouraged. Much progress has been realized. Illinet Online began using the Washington Library Network software in 1988; it provides full bibliographic records for the holdings of Illinet libraries. With links to circulation systems, it can be easily determined whether an item is checked out or what the holdings are for a title.

3. Reference/Information Services. The hierarchy for requesting materials and information includes local libraries, eighteen Public Library Systems, four Research and Reference Centers, and three Special Resource Centers. In FY 87, more than 325,000 interlibrary loan transactions were initiated (Sloane and Stewart 1988). And to counteract one of our professional myths, that the large libraries lend and the small libraries borrow, the largest library in the network was a net borrower that same fiscal year (p. 97).

4. Cooperative Collection Development. User-oriented collection development policies at the local level with some determination of collecting responsibilities at the system level are a priority.

5. Continuing Education. Historically, the emphasis for Illinet's continuing education programs has been on training users of OCLC's products and systems. They continue to provide that education and training. Individual library systems "support a variety of continuing education programs aimed at all levels of library staff" (La Croix 1987, p. 24). The accomplishments of Illinet and Illinois librarians are impressive. Undergirding this library evolution, however, is the major premise adopted by Illinois legislators and citizens, and that is "Access to information is a right, not a privilege."

I've briefly described two statewide, state-supported library networks, NAAL in Alabama and Illinet in Illinois. The overarching purpose of each is to improve the availability of information and documents to library users. It may be stated somewhat differently and the specific programs to achieve that goal may be prioritized differently, but all the *means* we've examined are focused toward that end.

CONCLUSION

We do have choices. Among them is the option to group ourselves for more effective information delivery and to seek funding from our state legislatures. That makes sense to me because of our collective strength, the benefit to library users, and the evident conclusion that we really are more than merely the sum of our parts. With the proliferation of information sources, we are long past the point when an individual institution or city can meet all the information needs of a scholar, a businessperson, a student, or the general citizen. The solution to our funding inadequacy may not be quickly or easily identified and procured—and not, perhaps, from a single source. In my opinion, only the most persuasive plan clearly communicated to decision makers will be seriously considered. We are competing with other community assets and services equally desperate for funding.

I prefer a multitype library network. An Illinet veteran tells of the jubilation on the University of Illinois campus when access was gained (and holdings information made available) from the John Deere Tractor Co. in Moline. Because they were marketing their tractors in China, they had amassed a significant corporate library collection on Chinese agriculture. Few knew about it, however, until the catalog records were added to the OCLC database.

The times are changing and user demands are accelerating. The expanding workforce of knowledge workers wants more information—and they want today's information, not yesterday's. Toffler (1990) describes the Marxist view that power flows to those who own the means of production such as a machine or a toolbox or a factory. Today's means of production lie inside the worker's head. It's brainpower. And libraries possess much of the raw material needed for that brain to function and generate new knowledge. This is "where society will find the single most important source of future wealth and power" (p. 217).

Florida's State Aid

James M. Wheeler
Director
Volusia County Public Library
Daytona Beach, Florida

What is the State of Florida?

Well, we're the fourth largest state in population, after California, New York, and Texas, just ahead of Pennsylvania, Illinois, and Ohio. Our 12.8 million population became one-third larger during the past decade.

However, we're not prosperous; our average annual income of $21,032 (what we pay a beginning librarian) is well under the United States average of $23,602. New York is at $28,873, California follows at $26,180, Illinois at $25,312—even Georgia's average is $1,000 more than Florida's.

Neither do we tax our people much. Our $983 per capita for all state taxes is $200 less than the national average; California, New York, and New Jersey hit you with $1,400. *Money* magazine (January 1991) calls Florida a tax haven.

Related to libraries, Florida spends $26.4 million on acquisitions. New York Public Library and libraries in Brooklyn and Queens spend over $30 million. The city of Pittsburgh spends one-half of what the whole state of Florida spends.

What do we excel at? Well, our dropout rate of 38.5 percent ranks us 48th in the number of kids completing high school; only Louisiana, the District of Columbia, and Mississippi graduate a smaller percentage. Do we get what we pay for? Our expenditure per pupil is $5,051; the U.S. average is $4,890; New York spends $8,094. Yet we spend more than California, $4,598.

Where do the young people go? With 40,000 prisoners, we have six percent of the nation's total. Yet we're 48th in population aged 18–34, and 49th in number of college degrees granted. We have one public university for every 1.4 million residents.

New York has one university for every 345,000 residents, Georgia has one for every 365,000 residents. Contributing to the worst high school graduation rate is that overall we rank 45th of the 50 states and the District of Columbia in juvenile incarceration, infant mortality, death rates for youngsters of 15 to 19, teenage out-of-wedlock birth rates, and the percentage of children living in poverty.

Should we even be talking about state aid to libraries? Where are our priorities?

When Governor Chiles was in Washington as chairman of the Senate Budget Committee, he proposed, to no avail, a $1 billion Healthy Bird Act for universal access to health care for pregnant mothers. He hopes to accomplish this in Florida, while cutting the HRS budget by $30.3 million.

In total public library expenditures we rank sixth. Remember, we are fourth in population (after California, New York, and Texas). New Jersey, ninth in population, is fifth in public library expenditures. Illinois, fourth in funding, is sixth in population.

Where is the peace dividend—the $68 billion science budget included $41 billion in military projects. The $15 billion energy budget included $4.4 billion for cleaning up the government's seventeen nuclear weapons plants. Forty-seven million dollars has been cut from mandatory entitlement social programs.

Just when our Florida state and local governments are *right-sizing* or *downsizing,* the federal government wants a return to state control of $21 billion in federal programs including grants for food stamps, sewage plants, public housing, and—their term—*library subsidies.* Footnote: In five years, states would begin paying for these programs. With Florida's needs in infrastructure and social programs now, where do you think L.S.C.A. (Library Service and Construction Act)-type programs will rank for funding, even if the state library has a Library Development Bureau left to administer the programs?

Anyone could present the history of state aid to libraries in Florida by researching the back issues of *Florida Libraries, Florida Statutes,* and information papers from the state library, such as the one State Librarian Barratt Wilkins prepared—"The Role of State Aid in the Florida Plan for Public Library Development."

There are sixty-three counties receiving state aid. I've been with one county for ten years. But I think my contribution has its basis in the company kept during the 1980s with the Florida Library Association.

My special knowledge comes from association with Rep. Sam Bell, author of perhaps the most controversial attempt to secure a source of dedicated funding for state aid to libraries. This was the Public Library Financial Assistance Act of 1986, which imposed a two percent tax on the sale or transfer of printed materials and book audio tapes, with appropriate exemptions for newspapers, textbooks, religious publications, political and campaign literature, and advertisements.

Despite impressive sponsorship, the bill died in committee. A newspaper account, always equating Sam Bell with a gunfighter in a white hat, said that he walked away into the sunset, but good authority said he left the committee hearing room, went back to his office, and asked staff for a list of bills submitted by the opposing legislators. As chairman of the House Appropriations Committee, he had a full gunbelt for sharpshooting against the bad guys.

Sam would have liked a "stump tax," a tax on trees cut for paper manufacturing, but political realities of the forest products industry controlling half the land in Florida limited this to just conversation in his office on Friday, December 6, 1985, at 10:30 A.M.

Another distinction for Volusia County related to state aid is the test lawsuit of 1977 brought against the county by the city of Ormond Beach. It claimed that the city received no real benefit from the county library system, that they were being doubly taxed for one service (a county-wide ad valorem tax for library operation and a city tax for their library, which had withdrawn from the federated county system after they received LSCA construction grants on their new building), and that the county was illegally performing a city function. Three years later, the city lost the suit, appealed, and rejoined the county system. The city library board chairman, who had worried that service would decline under the county, was appointed to the county board and became our most effective advocate.

In 1963, we also seemed to be the point man for counties not keeping state aid in a separate "county fee library fund." It was alleged that the county had misappropriated $18,450 in state aid. We retaliated against our county commission as much as against the state with a Special Bill for Volusia County providing for state aid and all library funds to be under the control of a County Library Board. Verna Nistendirk of the State Library wished us well, but gently pointed out that we would be ineligible for federal and state funds if we did not keep a separate fund. Our special bill thankfully died, but I wonder why all the attention was paid to Volusia County.

Going further back, to 1961, I was amazed to find in my inherited files that chairman George C. Boone, Jr., of our County Library Committee was an outstandingly effective lobbyist for the library development bill. In his files was a speech given by a member of the House Appropriations Committee from Daytona Beach, Frederick B. Karl, on central Florida television in early 1961 that gives us an outstanding technique for building advocacy:

> Last fall I was asked to speak to a regional meeting of a group of people who are interested in public libraries. I was asked to discuss a proposed legislative act dealing with public libraries which would provide grants to the various counties qualifying. . . . I explained to the people who attended the meeting that the procedure they had used to make me, as their State Representative, familiar with this proposed legislation was one of the most effective methods I had ever seen employed. Instead of sending a delegation to me to explain the proposed legislation and ask me to support it, they simply asked me to speak on the subject as though I knew all there was to know about it. Needless to say, I had never read the proposed bill, I did not know the details of the State's situation relating to public libraries and I, therefore, found myself in a situation where I was required to do considerable research before I could even carry on an intelligent discussion of the subject which had been assigned to me. As I realized what had happened to me, I became amused and very interested and I did engage in rather extensive research to see what I could find out about this particular problem of the State of Florida.

In 1970, Senator Karl was a leader in doubling state aid and appropriating planning funds for the State Library Building. Even then state aid only equalled 7 1/2 cents per capita compared to Georgia's 61 cents, but we were up to one volume per capita.

An interesting custom in 1971 was that the grant checks were handed to Florida legislators by the secretary of state, who said he felt that the legislators, whose votes made the funds possible, would appreciate being given the opportunity to hand the checks over to the county commissioners and library officials. Today, I'm sure our governing officials would sneer and ask if this were a 50 percent down payment on our full entitlement.

We think our 46,000 Library Friends and Trustees are active now. Well, we're political neophytes compared to the 1964 Friends and Trustees and the old Library Commission.

They sent a letter to Mr. Karl that began, "A gubernatorial candidate is needed who will be concerned enough about Florida's inadequate State Library, and Florida's inadequate public libraries to make their improvement and expansion a part of his campaign platform.

"The candidate for governor who makes the library program a part of his campaign platform will, I believe, be history's first to champion public libraries. Thousands of voters in the Florida Library Association, the Friends of the Library organizations, the Florida Federation of Women's Clubs, the Florida Congress of Parents and Teachers, men's service clubs and others working for libraries are hoping for such a candidate."

FLA then followed up with invitations to all candidates to speak ten minutes to 300 library Trustees and Friends at their annual banquet, asking for an abstract of the candidate's remarks to send to the newspapers throughout the state.

When do you remember first learning about state aid to public libraries?

Was it the page and a half in the 1962 Wheeler & Goldhor's *Practical Administration of Public Libraries?* The authors reported that about half the states have such aid. They deduced that state aid is best used to effect a balance between resources available in various areas and to stimulate local effort. This was of vital importance, as even in 1962 they saw the effects on libraries of the increased tax load on real property.

Did Florida's 1961 plan distribution formula recognize the differences between areas both in their taxable wealth and in the effort made to raise funds locally? Yes, with the equalization grants. Did it encourage local expenditure? Yes, with operating grants of 25 percent of local funds expended.

Ann Prentice (1977) quoted Ralph Blasingame's 1970 "Critical Analysis of State Aid Formulas" (*Library Trends* 19:252) where he said that state agencies spurred by the requirements of L.S.C.A. made the following policy decisions:

> Stimulation of local public library support
>
> Equalization of opportunity between rich and poor areas
>
> Relief of the local tax load
>
> Provision for "richer" local public library programs
>
> Recognition that state government has a responsibility to support the flow of information

PLACES RATED ALMANAC

I'm sure you ran to this in 1985 and found that libraries were ranked among *the arts.*

You'll recall that the mystic formula was Reading Quotient—a rough indicator of reading habits—the number of volumes added to circulation and divided by population served. The author's conclusions were that this Reading Quotient favored small or medium-sized metropolitan areas in New England and the northwest Midwest, for example, Bangor, Maine; Pittsfield, Massachusetts; Madison, Wisconsin; and Duluth, Minnesota.

As five of the metropolitan areas with the lowest reading quotients were in the South—notably for us, Fort Lauderdale, Pompano, Hollywood—the authors concluded that climate may be a partial reason that time spent reading increases as "ideal" outdoor weather decreases. However, Monterey, California, was in the high list, and Canton, Ohio, was the lowest.

In putting it all together in the best metropolitan areas, the library correlation seemed to be only in size of library, that is, number of volumes. Here we find, for instance, Pittsburgh, Boston, Philadelphia, St. Louis, and Dallas.

For the 1989 edition of *Places Rated Almanac*, the rating system changed to Public Library Acquisitions, expressed in the number of new books added per 10,000 residents. Two hundred three new books per 10,000 residents (in the 277 public libraries within metropolitan New York) equals 203 points. Point scores are, for example, 50 points for a museum, 100 points for a PBS station, one point for each weekly hour of radio programming for classical or concert music.

Now we find such turnarounds as Canton, Ohio, rising from lowest place in 1985 to twelfth in 1989, and Monterey, California, dropping slightly, from ninth to twelfth.

The "worst" list consists predominantly of towns and cities in Texas. Lakeland–Winter Haven, in Polk County, Florida (the eighth most populous county in Florida and one of only six without county library systems), is twelfth from the bottom, acquiring only 11,401 books for their 405,382 population.

Whatever happened to the ALA standard of two to four books per capita with new titles of at least 5 percent of the collection purchased annually?

Is it any wonder that Florida public libraries are spending 81.5 percent of their state aid on library materials, compared with 16.84 percent of our total operating expenditures? Altogether, we've added 625,361 books annually to our 17.5 million—1.38 per capita—up a very modest .02. In twenty-five years, we'll reach the two books per capita target.

What pitfalls await library directors after they receive their state aid appropriations? I often hear from library directors, "My county

73

wants to lower the library budget by the amount of state aid received. What can I do?"

I remind them that state aid is based on local expenditures; lowering your appropriation will directly affect the amount of future state aid—the future being two years hence, when statistically a higher pro rata share can be expected.

There are other strategies for coping:

1. Low-ball the state aid revenue estimate in next year's budget
2. If your expenditures are rising, use state aid as a carryover reserve; as it is received in late spring when you're putting your budget together for FY beginning October 1, show it as next year's revenue. Simply stated, this is a problem, because state aid applications must show the deductions for the year the state aid was received, not the year it was spent.
3. After you've underestimated the amount to be received, give your governing body a spending plan for the surplus. Treat it as a grant; show that you need to use it for a specific position or equipment or something like Magazine Index or Newsbank.

In support of Florida, I commend the Growth Management Act of 1985. The idea behind the creation of this act was that Florida has been sold too cheaply and has grown too haphazardly. There can be impact fees, as much as $5,000 on a new home, for roads, sewers, parks, and fire service. Some counties have extended this to libraries, for the building space and books per capita needed to maintain a set level of service, such as .39 square feet and 1.82 books per capita.

And our new population, over three million people in the 1980s, came from states that had better libraries, states such as New York, Ohio, Massachusetts, New Jersey, Illinois. With a 43 percent population growth rate, or 110,000 more people, in my county, we have found support for doubling our library budget while library space tripled, circulation doubled, and the number of professional positions went from ten to sixty-three.

The 1980s also brought another crisis of conscience. Our state organization of Friends of the Library asked the FLA to lobby for a sales tax exemption for Friends. This would exempt Friends' activities such as book sales, dinners, bookbags, and other fund-raisers. We were asking for more state aid money and they were reluctant to support the effort.

In a masterful piece of legislative legerdemain, the Tallahassee twist, or Sam Bell spin, gave librarians the clout we needed over our Friends to pry loose their funds and direct them to our needs.

The law (F.S. 212.0821) states that the legislative intent is that public libraries use their sales tax exemptions for purchase of necessary goods and services requested by groups solely engaged in fundraising activities for such libraries. Ergo, since the library was spending the Friends' funds, these also qualified as a local expenditure qualifying for state aid.

What victories have been won in state aid? We peaked in 1990, with appropriations at their highest level—$17.3 million, which translates to 11.3 cents per local dollar. The appropriation is all from recurring funds. Following trust funds, recurring funds are the best kind, which means in a rising economy you can expect they will be there next year. But all bets were off in 1991; the state has a shortfall of $1.4 billion and a budget of $28.8 billion.

The solution: Use some of the money from the state lottery, arguing that public libraries qualify as an educational enhancement to public schools. If that doesn't work (on our second and third try) well, then there may be a casino gambling bill. Our local dog track and jai-alai and off-track wagering hasn't given any funds to the library—let's get in on the action with casinos.

The groundwork for use of lottery funds was laid in 1987, with the following letter from Florida Secretary of State George Firestone to all legislators:

Florida's public libraries are educational institutions and should be funded as such.

- Public libraries are open longer hours and on more days than any other educational institution.
- Public libraries have the largest enrollment of any of the state's educational programs (26 percent of the state's population).
- Public libraries are the principal source of education for youth after school hours, on weekends, and during the summer.
- Public library users report that 33 percent of their 35 million annual visits are for educational purposes and after 3:00 P.M., the percentage rises to nearly 60 percent.
- Public library users under age 18 report more than 50 percent of their visits are for educational purposes.
- Public libraries provide over one-third of the volunteer literacy programs in Florida.

These are just some of the facts found on pp. 12 and 13 of the pamphlet *Libraries Improve Florida's Education: A report on the role of public libraries in the education of Florida's children and illiterate adults.* This report represents the first data on an important aspect of public education which has been long assumed but not verified.

To fully fund our State Aid to Libraries Law would take an additional $16 million over the current $7.6 million provided. It is a small investment with a large cost-effective and cost-efficient return. I wish we had more state-aided programs with such a broad benefit to children and illiterate adults.

In any event, Al Trezza became president of FLA in July 1991 and as he wrote the 1985 Florida Standards for Public Library Service, it's his job to come up with the $2.25 *minimum* per capita in state aid, an increase of the $11 million he set for us.

PART 3

Samuel Lazerow Memorial Lecture

The Economic Impact of Information: Implications for Libraries

Patricia Glass Schuman
President
American Library Association, Chicago, Illinois

President
Neal Schuman, Publishers, Inc., New York, New York

In our society information is a resource at least as important as energy. Sometimes it's regarded as a commodity to be bought and sold. Sometimes it's viewed as a building block for economic development. At other times, we value information as a "public good" essential for a democratic society—a good that should be available to all. The question is not so much about "free" information; there is always cost. The basic questions are: Who will pay? And who will benefit?

Of course, neither the need for information, nor its value, is a new phenomenon. What is new is the amount of information an individual requires to negotiate the complex social and economic structures of the modern world. The power of information to determine who will do well and who will do poorly is unprecedented.

Information-age, post-industrial economy, knowledge society—these are the dominant metaphors of the '80s and '90s. We are told that our economy is no longer dependent on raw materials, that we now live in a society powered by information. Our early ancestors hoped to shape the future with magic. We now believe we can shape destiny with information. The modern incantations are efficiency, manageability, rationality, value, and impact.

The information society metaphor is simplistic. It can lead us, if we are not careful, to adopt the agenda of the marketplace rather than to forge our own. From the first time someone offered "a penny for your thoughts"—a phrase that can be traced back to at least the sixteenth century—people have tried to put a value on information. But neither a penny nor a million pennies can truly buy any of our thoughts as we think them. We must not confuse the transmission of data or facts with the use people make of them.

Certainly, the ways we use data and information to formulate knowledge and wisdom does have economic impact and far-reaching implications for libraries. But how can we judge this impact? How can we affect it? Our judgments, and our effects, very much depend on how we as a profession value information.

Oscar Wilde once described a cynic as "someone who knows the cost of everything, and the value of nothing." Librarians cannot afford to be cynical about information. We are, after all, members of a profession steeped in the values of democracy. We must keep these in mind when we consider conflicting values, like *fee* or *free.*

Basically, when the economics of information are discussed, three prevalent value questions emerge: Should we value information as a market commodity? Should we value information as a crucial building block for economic growth and development? Is information a vital force we can use to help create a just and humane society?

The choices we make about these three values, how much weight we give each of them, will have major implications for how the information society we speak of so often will survive the so-called information deluge.

Take the first value: Information is a commodity to be bought and sold in the marketplace like any other product. Conventional economic wisdom tells us that the production and distribution of commodities are best handled by a competitive economic system. Demand is measured by how much people are willing to pay. This leads to the best allocation of resources based on what people want.

The mythology of the free market economy has been pervasive since the days of Adam Smith. The hero of the free market myth is competition, aided by the marketplace's "invisible hand." Competition's quest is for efficiency and diversity through free enterprise. Competition's rallying cry is: "If you keep big government off my back, I will preserve free choice." Competition's boast is: "Information, our most crucial capital resource, is a precious commodity. Only I, Competition, can nurture it! Only I, Competition, can make sure it will flourish. Only I, Competition, can guarantee prosperity, diversity, and choice."

The free market myth is enticing. But information in and of itself is not a pure market commodity that can simply be bought or sold. When I buy a tank of gas, I pay the attendant and the gas belongs to me. Sooner than I would like, I use up the gas. When I buy a book or a CD-ROM, I buy only the container. Both the seller and I now have the information contained therein. When we buy or sell traditional commodities, ownership changes hands. The seller gives up possession to the buyer. That is not true of information. Information often becomes more valuable when it is shared.

The free market scenario is based on the premise that there are standardized products about which consumers have perfect information to make decisions about purchases. But if I have perfect information about information, I have no need to buy it. Certainly, information products like books, databases, and periodicals can certainly add shape and value to information. As a publisher who hopes to continue to make a living by adding value, I count on that. But doesn't it seem rather comical to pay for a database search according to how long one has been on-line with a computer, rather than on the value of what the search produces?

Free marketeers equate value with profit. And there are certainly high profits to be made by selling some information, particularly if the U.S. government, the world's largest compiler of information, gets out of the information dissemination business.

The largest costs for the information producer are creation and compilation, not transmission. Why else would the Information Industry Association (IIA) fight so hard to keep the U.S. government from "adding value" to the large amounts of data it collects at taxpayer expense? "Adding value" is the current euphemism for making electronic databases usable by the public; the IIA wants to leave that part to the private sector.

Convincing the public to view information as a commodity is a high stakes game with powerful players. The few media moguls who control the field know that information is power, especially when one controls both the source and the transmission. The growing media monopolies are operating in an environment similar to the early laissez-faire days of the big oil companies. The Robert Maxwells and the Rupert Murdochs own the "wells, the trucks, and the pumps." What the free market proponents of information as a commodity conveniently ignore is that there is really very little competition in the information marketplace. Much of the benefit claimed for privatization of government information depends upon competition encouraging companies to lower prices and improve quality. If privatization amounts to nothing more than trading a public monopoly for a private one, little has been accomplished.

Ben Bagdikian has chronicled the takeover of information companies by a handful of multinational interlocking media conglomerates, conglomerates with chief executive officers like the late Robert Maxwell, who proudly announced his goal to be one of "ten surviving global information companies." Project Censored chose Bagdikian's *Nation* article "The Lords of the Global Village" as one of the top ten censored stories of 1990.[1] Similarly, ALA's continuing chronicle detailed increasing cutbacks and privatization, "Less Access to Less Information by and about the U.S. Government" was chosen by Project Censored as a top ten censored story, two years in a row.[2]

"Competition!" may be the rallying cry of the commoditiers, but the reality is concentration in the private sector. This is a far cry from nurturing the diversity of information sources that "competition" promises, a far cry from counteracting potential government control. A handful of companies—mostly foreign owned—now control traditional publishing houses. Five vendors, three of whom are foreign owned or controlled, control 90 percent of the database market. Fewer than fifteen companies control our major newspapers. It's hardly surprising that the Bagdikian and ALA stories aren't published in the mainstream media.

Some of these corporations have revenue streams and economic power far greater than many nations. They are competing in a race to control the world's media outlets. They lobby hard for privatization of our public information assets. Their goal is not to further democracy; their goal is to maximize profits.

Remember, the term *commodity* is an economic concept, and economics is a social science. Sometimes it's even called the "dismal science." Ironically, the entry "Economics of Uncertainty and Information" was added as a category to the American Economic Association Classification for Articles and Abstracts in 1976, just about the time Daniel Bell and others began to talk about a post-industrial society powered by information.

The information society does not replace, it overlaps. Placing the highest value on information as a market commodity can be misleading, even dangerous. It can lead us to adopt what Vincent Mosco calls the "pay-per-use" society. Valuing information as a commodity leads us to possible contradictions. Information just doesn't fit the true commodity mold.

What about the second value: Information is a building block for economic growth and development. Again, we must not overlook the subtleties. We must not fall into what some bankers now call the "MBA mentality": Mexico, Brazil, and Argentina. This is the trap of looking for short-term profits while disregarding solid, long-term investment. After all, the cost of information is often independent of the scale of its use. A given piece of information—a stock price, a scientific discovery—costs the same to acquire whether the decision to be based on it is large or small. Research leading to the treatment of AIDS will cost the same whether it is used to help one hundred or one hundred thousand patients. The value, the impact, is vastly different.

Consider, for example, the increases in the costs of information to businesspeople or to farmers when government databases are privatized. Statistical, commodity, and other agricultural reports used to be available at no or low cost in print formats through the government printing office. Thousands of these were eliminated during the Reagan Administration's "war on waste." There is an agricultural database that used to be available free from the USDA or for $50 a year plus 50 cents a minute from a nonprofit service; it has now been contracted out to Martin Marietta. The database is still free to Martin Marietta, but anyone else must pay them $150 a month plus $45 an hour, or $96 an hour to DIALOG.[3]

It is hard to define exactly where the line between public and private goods lies, but it is obvious that many information products and services have some of the characteristics of public goods. A public good is traditionally thought of as something that benefits many people and is paid for collectively. Consumption by one person does not reduce the amount available to others. The lighthouse is the classic example; its beam is available to all ships as a beacon to guide them to shore. Use of the light by one ship's pilot does not reduce the amount of light available to others. Anyone can use it. It's paid for collectively. Other typical examples include highways, schools, police, firefighters, and national defense and security.

Viewing information as a building block for economic development—a true public good—rather than merely as a tradeable commodity, means making distinctions. We must distinguish between information products, information services, and information systems; between information providers and the content of information. The true function of information is as a catalyst. Information adds value. It has economic impact because it increases the overall value of other resources.

Libraries of all kinds can play a crucial role in that process. M-Link, a partnership between the University of Michigan libraries and seven small rural public libraries in the state, is an excellent example of the possibilities. M-Link's goal is to equalize access to economic community development information by providing remote access to the collections and trained personnel of the sixth largest research library in the United States. The project supplies the smaller libraries with public access computers, fax machines, software, and training.

Another example is the Carnegie Library of Pittsburgh's Neighborline, a community and economic development service designed to help small business people and community groups solve social and economic problems. The Long Island Business and Education Partnership, initiated by the Nassau County Library System, has launched seminars, job fairs, and job hotlines.

Across the country librarians are providing services to help people use and share resources to their fullest potential. This is essential. We may be surrounded by an abundance of data. But it is not a given that we are rich with information, much less knowledge or wisdom. It very likely means that we are swamped.

There are over fifty articles on my desk that might relate to my presidential theme, "Your Right To Know: Librarians Make It Happen." I haven't had time to read them. No doubt, they may contain information I need. The fact that I haven't yet read the current brochures about where to invest my IRA by April 15 can certainly have economic impact. The data has been organized by someone, and I have easy access to it. I simply haven't used it. It's doing me no good! And, of course, I feel guilty.

More important, books, magazines, and most other information products and services are not of any use to people who cannot read. Information cannot be used until we receive it in some organized way. It cannot do us any good unless we are intellectually able—and psychologically motivated—to use it. Even then, we must first take the time to internalize it and integrate it with everything else we know.

Information is not a true commodity. We should value it as a good that can help maximize resources and further economic development. But even more crucial, we must value information as an essential resource to a humane and just society. Here is where information has its greatest value, its force, its maximum economic impact, and its most crucial implications as a public good.

Consider, for example, the Community Right to Know Act passed by Congress in 1986. It mandates that all manufacturing plants complete an annual Toxic Chemical Release Inventory Form indexing the kind and amount of toxic chemicals they discharge into the air, land, and water.

Though the TRI database has only been publicly available since June 1989, it has already had tremendous impact. Investigative reporters have written stories based on the information, and citizen organizations have prepared their own reports on industrial polluters. These reports alone have stimulated passage of new state and local laws, and created a virtual revolution in industry attitudes. Companies have made voluntary commitments to cut back sharply and ultimately eliminate toxic pollutants.

What's most exciting is that information about community toxic air emissions is now as close as the local library. The EPA has provided libraries nationwide with microfiche copies of the TRI, plus fact sheets on pollutants. Some have charged that the costs for the government to produce and disseminate such information is too high. But what is the cost of pollution to our planet if our government does not make such information widely available?

Gains in economic productivity require a healthy, flexible, educated, and informed populace. We know that investments in human resources are crucial, yet in our society such investment has a low priority, lower than industrial, agricultural, or military expenditures.

Project Head Start, for example, a program directed at helping "high-risk" children, saves $4.75 in welfare and prison costs for every $1 spent—but it's funded to reach only 18 percent of eligible children. We need $2 billion more to reach every eligible child. Meanwhile, we add one million illiterate teenagers every year to our already shockingly high number of nonreaders. The high school drop-out rate is now around 30 percent. Fifty percent of all black 17-year-olds are functionally illiterate, fifteen percent of graduates from urban high schools read at lower than 6th-grade level. More than 33 percent of mothers receiving Aid to Families with Dependent Children are illiterate. With twenty-three million Americans unable to read or write at the eighth grade level, adult illiteracy is a national disaster.

Some economists estimate that illiteracy costs more than $200 billion per year in lost productivity, welfare payments, crime, accidents, and lost taxes. Nevertheless, the United States, based on a percentage of the GNP, ranks only sixth in spending for public education, out of the world's eleven largest nations. And in 1991 the Bush Administration recommended only $45 million to fund Department of Education library programs.

The simple truth is that we will not live in a true information society unless—and until—we ensure that people have access to information and cultural content. We will not live in a true information society until we have a populace with the skills and resources to use this content. The right to know is embedded in our constitution. The right to know is much more than just free speech. Free expression requires not only Constitutional guarantees but certain educational ones as well. If you have no education, no job, and no property, your voice doesn't carry very far.

You may have the right to know, but if you don't know how to use it, you may not even be aware of it. As commentator George Will points out: "AIDS is not a democratic disease threatening us all equally. AIDS is behaviorally based. It's hard to get, and easy to prevent. Easy, that is, if information is heeded, which it is by advantaged people."[4]

Information is the basis for communication. The communication capabilities of individuals—their "literacy"—will largely determine the benefits they receive from an information society. More than any other one factor it was this country's decision to offer free public education and free public libraries that enabled the American people to prosper. But today, growing numbers live in poverty. Poor people are as cut off from information as they are from money.

To have positive effects on the economy the library profession must reject the view that information is a commodity. We must recognize that information is essential to economic development, crucial to a just social agenda. If we truly accept the words carved above the portals of many libraries that "knowledge is power," then with our knowledge as a profession comes a responsibility for the exercise of power. We must understand that efficiency means doing something right. Effectiveness means we do the right thing.

In his poem "The Rock," T. S. Eliot asks the question we must ask ourselves: "Where is the wisdom we have lost in knowledge?/ Where is the knowledge we have lost in information?" Libraries hold data and information in trust for the public, so that people may use them to create wisdom and knowledge.

The economists call us "a service industry." But as New York Public Library president Timothy Healy points out, "The simple word 'service' just won't do . . . we exist to serve freedom."[5] Fees for services may provide some short-term funds. Ultimately they will impoverish our institutions and our profession.

The business of libraries is not information. Libraries have no business in business. The mission of librarians is understanding through knowledge. We are weapons in the information society's "arsenal of democracy." We are part of the solution to problems like illiteracy and unemployment. Our information services can help businesses to prosper, students to learn, and adults to discover. The library is one of the few institutions where a child's question is treated as seriously as an adult's, where a 6-year-old's request for "a picture of a dog" is considered as important as a businessperson's need for demographic information.

Librarians are part of a profession dedicated to making everyone's "Right to Know" happen. To paraphrase a recent *Economist* article: Far from being the keepers of dusty storehouses, over-whelmed by the deluge of information, librarians can be the pilots of the lifeboats, helping society set course for an equitable, enlightened, ethical information age.[6]

NOTES

1. Ben Bagdikian, "The Lords of the Global Village," *The Nation* (1987): 805–820.

2. *Less Access to Less Information by and about the U.S. Government: A 1981–1990 Chronology* (Washington, DC: American Library Association Washington Office).

3. Nancy Kranich, "Information Drought: Next Crisis for the American Farmer?" *Library Journal*, 114(1989): 22–27.

4. George Will, "Information Age Has Left the Poor Behind," *Oakland Tribune*, January 8, 1989.

5. Timothy S. Healy, "Libraries in Service to Democracy," Keynote Address, NYLA Centennial Conference, New York, 1990.

6. "The World's Greatest Libraries: Arks from the Deluge," *The Economist*, 313(1989): 41–47.

PART 4

Local Funding of Academic and Public Libraries

Local Funding of
Public Libraries

Marjorie Turnbull
County Commissioner
Leon County, Florida

I would like to put the conference theme, "The Funding of Public and Academic Libraries: The Critical Issue for the '90s," in the context of local government. In doing so I want to address two realities: the world within which you are operating at the local level and the constraints you face, and the world you want to accomplish in spite of these constraints.

Let me tell you a bit about county government, because skills needed to accomplish your goals at this level of government are different from those needed at the state or federal level. Understanding the organizational context within which you are working is vital to success.

Counties are constitutional creatures of the state—the local arm of the state—originally set up to handle the judiciary system. Over the years the county's role has expanded as the demands of the state have increased so that we now have the responsibility for a broad range of services, including roads, environmental protection, solid waste management, public health, and so on.

First of all, county government, until recently, was run by the commissioners themselves. Cities, historically throughout the century, have relied on an administrative staff to carry out their functions. Counties have developed a similar need as the complexity of their responsibilities has expanded. As an example, Leon County did not have a county administrator until 1974. The City of Tallahassee has had a city manager since 1919.

Second, a county commission has both legislative and executive powers. Unless specifically provided for in a charter, you do not have a separation of powers at the county level as you do at state and federal. This means we both appropriate the dollar and spend it. The practical impact here is that local decisionmakers have no place to hide—and no place to spread the blame. We cannot appropriate the money and then accuse the executive branch of misusing our well-intentioned appropriation. In like manner, as the executive branch, we cannot "blame" the legislature for its failure to appropriate sufficient funds to carry out the job.

Another significant consideration about county government is that we are in session 365 days a year. We do not go off to the state capital or Washington and make our decisions, then come home to face the public, often weeks after the decision is made. The response to our decisions is known and immediate. We do not have the luxury of time and distance to temper the reaction to our decisions. Local government is not a haven for the timid!

Superimposed on these organizational realities is a set of funding realities, which also must be recognized if we are to be successful in making our case to local government.

The last decade witnessed tremendous changes that have increased the fiscal demands of county government. Federal and state government are shifting more and more responsibility to the local level without shifting the revenue to support these responsibilities. In November 1990, Florida passed a constitutional amendment to make this practice by the state more difficult. This amendment provided that if the state is going to mandate that local government perform a task, then it must also provide funding for that task. The prohibition of this requirement can be overruled by a two-thirds vote of the legislature.

Urbanization has brought with it an increased demand for services. Some counties operate like cities as the provider of urban services. This means that counties are not just reacting to state mandates for services but local demands as well and libraries are one of these services.

The public's expectations of government have substantially increased in the last two decades; government is viewed as the place where problems should be solved.

Overriding these realities is the very real constraint of the local revenue base. The ability to fund programs adequately is a greater problem for counties than for any other level of government. Certainly in Leon County we are highly dependent on the property tax, one of the most regressive taxes and one that meets the most resistance from the public. Taxpayer response to a proposed increase in the property tax is very direct and immediate.

Unlike the state and federal government, we are where the buck stops. We have nowhere else to which to pass down our costs. The Florida legislature, and I suspect others, is suggesting that the solution to this problem is to give local governments more flexibility in increasing taxes, such as doing away with referenda and the like. Don't be fooled by this. This is not the solution. In fact, it may set up a chain of conditions that will make it harder and harder to raise revenue at every level of government. If the legislature lacks the political will to raise taxes, why should we expect local officials who eyeball their constituents on a daily basis to be more comfortable doing so?

Today's financial picture is grim. Truly it is the grimmest I can remember in a long series of grim years. Our ability to increase taxes under the current tax system in Florida is marginal. Absent a state income tax—which I do not believe we will see in our lifetime—the only serious option is a service tax. At the local level in Florida, most counties have reached their constitutional limitation of ten mills on the property tax.

Our commissioners recently had their first in a series of budget workshops in which we have had to face future cutbacks as a result of revenue shortfalls. So that you will understand the reality of the decisions we are making, here is a little example.

I am going to give you $100 to fund local government. There are several categories: (1) law enforcement, which includes the sheriff, court clerk, judges, state attorney, public defender, jail; (2) roads, which includes paving and maintenance; (3) environmental protection, which includes growth management, water quality protection, stormwater runoff management, land use, building permits; (4) public health, which includes the public health department, mental health programs, mosquito control; (5) solid waste management, which includes hazardous waste, operation of the land fill, garbage collection; (6) library. Now prioritize these categories and assign a dollar amount to these activities. You may be surprised to learn that in our county—and this is not unusual—law enforcement takes up $45 of every $100 we collect. Now let's assume a budget cut and take away $20. What will you cut? What lower level of service will you ask the citizens of this community to assume? And how will you convince them that this is in their best interest?

I think you see the dilemma. We aren't talking about fluff here. We aren't talking about doing away with something that does not need to be done. We are talking bone and gristle. We are talking about essential services without which it would be impossible to function in a civilized society.

You can see why libraries are in danger. You cannot tell someone "we aren't going to take care of your garbage because we have to run our library."

Now lest you think I am going to leave you with this gloom and doom scenario, let me move to the second part of my comments.

How then do you achieve what you want in spite of these constraints? How do you convince local government policymakers that, in spite of these immediate and urgent demands, libraries are not disposable items in a budget?

In Leon County we recently dedicated a brand-new public library. It is magnificent. I hope each of you will have a chance to visit it. The battle to achieve this new library is a lesson in how to convince policymakers that libraries are as essential to a civilized society as picking up its garbage.

Our new library is a testimony to the grit and resolve of a group of dedicated volunteers who simply would not give up. It isn't a short story. There were times when they must have relished the thought of giving up, having done all that was humanly possible and meeting obstacle after obstacle. But they didn't, and their results are evident.

The saga started in 1956 when Tallahassee founded its first library and thus gave up its distinction as the only state capital in the nation without a public library. Despite repeated attempts to find a permanent home over the next thirty years, our library grew in successive temporary housing.

Finally, in 1986, a group of citizens came together and formed project BUILD, dedicated to the proposition that this community was going to have a permanent central public library. They came to the commission and filled our chambers with children, adults, and balloons. There was resistance from a county commission that was facing, even then, enormous demands on its resources. They knew they were going to have to build a court-ordered jail, which alone might take all its discretionary dollars.

The message of the advocates had a shade of guilt overlying it; a "for shame commissioners" that we don't have a library we can be proud of. But most of all—and most important to their ultimate success—it was a message of hope and excitement. These volunteers said, "You do your part and we will do ours. We will not expect you to do this alone. If you appropriate the local dollars for the building, we will mobilize the private sector in the community to participate in funding the furnishings and the collections."

And they did it. The library is a testament to community involvement. There are those who purchased a room; there are those who purchased a paperback book. It did not matter what one's ability to give was—the Friends of the Library had an opportunity for you. Throughout this process, the Friends continually kept commissioners informed. At least every six months, I would get a call from a Friend wanting to brief me on where the Friends stood. They would ask for my input and this would leave me with a sense of excitement about what they were doing.

I could go on. The success of this effort was seen on opening day when we had 10,000 people come through the library. There has been a dramatic increase in the number of people taking out library cards. But the greatest tribute comes from the children who are discovering learning. A friend of mine has found that his 3-year-old likes to go to the library every Saturday morning to color. She just likes to color among the books. We were visited by a group of kindergarten children at our last county commission meeting. As you might expect, they were somewhat shy in speaking up or responding to our questions. Then one commissioner asked, "How many of you have visited our new public library?" Their expressions changed to visible excitement and every hand went up.

How does one relate to the rather gloomy scenario I presented earlier? Does all of this mean that our library will escape any cuts? Probably not. But it does mean that there is not a prayer's chance of our undermining what has already been presented to this community as a leap forward in our sense of ourselves as a community.

In the final analysis, you who lobby, prod, educate, badger, nag on behalf of libraries have *never* had it easy—even in the best of times. Yours is always an uphill battle of convincing policymakers that your services are essential. So you should be better prepared than most to fight the budget battles of the '90s. You will have to deal with the realities, to be prepared to accept new ideas and new approaches to both funding and providing services. Your key to success is in a willingness to involve the public and use volunteers in ways you never anticipated. In doing so you build a strong political base that is difficult to deny.

John Kennedy said: "The life of the arts, far from being an interruption, a distraction in the life of a nation, is close to the center of a nation's purpose—and is a test of the quality of a nation's civilization." The same could be said for libraries.

And that is your essential message.

Local Funding of Academic Libraries

Laurence Miller
Director
Florida International University
Miami, Florida

A look at academic library funding over the past fifteen years reveals both positive and negative aspects. On the positive side, academic library budgets have substantially outpaced the consumer price index.

Comparing projected 1988 figures with those of 1976, the CPI stood at 223.8, whereas academic library budgets stood at 258.5 for public institutions and 242.1 for private institutions. These are based on figures pulled together by John Budd in a *Library Administration & Management* article.[1]

The negative, of course, is not hard to find. During the period from 1976 to 1985, library budgets declined on the average from 5.05 to 3.73 as a percentage of educational and general expenditures in the institutions served.

Selsky, writing in *Library Journal*,[2] found that while libraries were using their budget increases to spend more on library materials, these increases had not kept pace with rising library materials cost. Not surprisingly, Budd found that expenditures for serials alone had increased from 11.8 percent to 16.6 percent of the budget in public institutions and from 10 percent to 14.1 percent in private academic libraries. He also estimated that by 1991, 20.5 percent of university library budgets would go for periodicals and only 10.6 percent for books.

I am sure that actual figures for the more recent period, for which statistics are not yet available, would be even more negative. For instance, the University of Virginia has indicated its intention to cut its journals list by $200,000 per year for the next four years. At a recent meeting of the Association of Southeastern Research Libraries, only the University of Kentucky was not planning any journals cuts.

In such an environment, all funding sources need to be examined closely. The degree of attention given to local funding varies dramatically from institution to institution. Obviously, private institutions receive almost all funding from local sources, but in state-supported academic libraries, the figures and commitment to exploiting local sources of income vary widely.

In other institutions, such as state university libraries requiring two to three million dollars each year for library resources, it is a matter of debate whether local sources of income and fund-raising activities represent, in any sense, the margin of excellence, except perhaps in the very long run. Nonetheless, this can be a source of real money. Paul Willis, library director at the University of Kentucky, indicates that the largest gift he ever received was a million dollars. He also spends 25 percent of his time in fund-raising activities.

Libraries have little in common when it comes to a discussion of how to attract a larger share of basic institutional appropriations. Funding mechanisms and personalities differ greatly and these, of course, have a major impact on funding approaches. This paper will therefore center on the types of local funding that both private and public university libraries have in common, including:

1. Local fundraising, including Friends groups
2. Income from local utilities, such as photocopiers
3. Fees

In view of current budget problems being experienced everywhere, it is appropriate that all library directors at least take a look at their fund-raising efforts and decide whether more time may be profitably spent in this activity.

In my view, conditions that argue in favor of organized fundraising activities include an effective university fundraising organization with which the library may cooperate; a well-developed and well-organized alumni effort; a tradition that enables the library to appeal to prestige; and the availability of staff, either within or outside the library, to supplement the efforts of the director in this area.

These conditions work against many younger public and private institutions: where alumni have not yet made and saved their first million dollars, where the alumni effort has not yet become a mature one, with well-developed mailing lists and a strong membership base, and in institutions where time is the most precious commodity, as valuable as money. But this is not to suggest that organized fund-raising activities should not be undertaken under these circumstances, especially when institutional loyalties of one type or another can be harnessed in a campaign.

A 1988 survey of ARL libraries (Z265. R45A85 no. 146) in which forty-eight libraries (86 percent of those queried) responded, found that there is a clear trend toward more organized efforts in the area of fundraising—efforts that go beyond Friends of the Library activities. In the words of the report, "Crucial factors that affect the outcome of fund-raising efforts are the nature and level of library support [for fund raising]; the library's relationship with the university's efforts; and the type of campaign strategy selected." The Office of Management Studies of ARL, which conducted the survey, found that most libraries employed one of three approaches:[3]

1. Assigned a current member of the library staff, or made a new appointment for this purpose (58 percent)
2. Had the dean or director assume responsibility (21 percent)
3. Depended primarily on the university's central development office (21 percent)

Seven libraries used consultants and eight used temporary staff. Most often (43 percent of the time), the expense was borne within the library budget.

Help commonly rendered by the parent institution included technical expertise (90 percent), mailing lists (69 percent), computing support (62 percent), personnel support (62 percent), and postage and mailing (24 percent).

Rated as most successful were campaigns focused on the improvement of the library's buildings and special collections.

Half the respondents considered that a general library component within a total university campaign is the most successful strategy. Not considering extreme variations, the mean goal of these campaigns was $5.98 million and the median, $4.5 million. While duration varied from one to six years, twenty-five libraries reported a mean of 3.5 years and a median of 4 years.

The three most commonly employed techniques were personal one-to-one appeals, direct mail, and presentations to groups. Eighty-eight percent targeted specific groups and reported that they were most successful with alumni and Friends of Libraries groups.

The report concludes:

The identification of targeted constituencies interested in supporting library causes and the establishment of communication with the education of these constituencies are important prerequisites to fund-raising and development campaigns. A library also needs to develop the ability to tell its stories of accomplishments and goals in meaningful and understandable ways to potential donors. A few libraries have obtained the support of public figures to help raise funds. In general, a strategy that includes personal contacts with individual donors on the part of the library director/dean or other spokesperson, along with well-developed and communicated campaigns, provides a sound basis for fundraising.

One valid objective of library fund-raising campaigns is to raise an endowment. Gregory Ritter briefly traversed some of the theoretical territory and the dynamics of fundraising campaigns in a presentation to the 1990 LAMA Preconference, "Implementing Successful Capital Campaigns for the Establishment of Endowment Funds in Libraries."[4] He indicated that the results of such campaigns when charted form a triangular pattern. These include a few major gifts at the tip, a larger group of smaller gifts in the midsection, and many small gifts at the base. Actual percentages may vary from one campaign and one development professional to the next, but the pattern holds true. Ritter's experience is that 3 percent of the gifts produce 25 percent of the total goal; that the next 10 percent yield 25 percent; the next 20 percent, 25 percent; and the final 67 percent, 25 percent. He argues that one of the major questions to be answered in determining the feasibility of whether you can undertake a successful *million-dollar* campaign is: Are there really three major donors whose potential gifts will add up to $250,000? He adds, "Some campaigns end before they begin, when this question is asked." In his view, the campaign budget should not exceed 5 to 10 percent of the goal and would typically allocate 80 percent to personnel costs and 10 percent each to promotion and office operation. One of the questions that I and many other library directors have faced is whether a Friends of the Library group fits into the overall development picture. At the ASERL meeting I have already referred to, attendees seemed evenly divided between those who had active friends groups; those who had moribund groups who either were considering, or were not planning to revitalize them; and those who neither had them nor were planning to establish them.

In a 1990 article in the library fundraising periodical *Bottom Line* entitled, "Starting a Development Office: One Academic Library's Experience," director David Laird and development officer Miriam Nickerson of the University of Arizona were interviewed by Susan Goldberg.[5] Nickerson cites a Friends group that, in her words, "does not want to do fundraising. They see themselves . . . primarily as a social organization. They didn't even want to increase their own membership and their own kitty." She adds, "After speaking to development officers in other libraries, I learned that this is a common problem."[6]

One library director who has a highly visible and, from the public relations standpoint, successful Friends group indicated that the Friends did little more than pay their way, though a major bequest from a member could change the balance sheet and the general picture. Friends can be used for a number of purposes, including heightening the library's profile within the academic community, contributing to the cultural life of the university, as well as fundraising. More typical functions include film or lecture series, literary lunches, and other activities that in many cases are of greater public relations than financial value.

Whatever the function, a high-profile Friends organization will be a time sponge until active lay leadership is recruited. Even when that milestone is reached, this is a time-consuming activity. Library administration must take the basic decision concerning whether the necessary time is available, and whether the potential financial benefits outweigh the commitment necessary to achieve success. In some cases, this decision may be preempted by the administration.

There are a number of other revenue sources for local funding of academic libraries. The really promising ones, however, are few.

In the entire roster of income producers, just one really stands out: photocopiers. At FIU, commissions paid to the university by our photocopy vender in 1990/91 exceeded $100,000. This is based on ten cents per copy. In a normal year (which this was not), the library would have expected to have returned half of this in the form of a super-adequate equipment budget. At the University of South Carolina, the income for the library was expected to reach $200,000. USC is its own entrepreneur, but we subcontract.

The photocopy function is so important, and so potentially profitable, that it is not one to be turned over to the administration, or to student government, and written off. The result is frequently poor service and, almost always, no money for the library.

With large numbers of students, the logistics of these operations are formidable and, given full-time and part-time enrollments of fifteen to twenty thousand students, at least one full-time individual is required on-site. If evenings and weekends are busy, more help is required. Based on our experience, vendors can either cut down on the logistical headaches of machines and paper or increase them depending on the responsibility, knowledge, and experience of the supplier selected. A general caveat is the well-known fact that in hard times institutions have a tendency to reduce library budgets in consideration of revenue sources such as this.

There is another quite controversial local funding source, namely fees for specific library services. Most of us have had to charge for on-line searching. In most cases, this is no better than a wash from the revenue point of view. Certainly, many libraries could not have provided these services—so necessary to keep library information functions current—on a fee basis. But we have done so with the knowledge that fees automatically make these services more accessible to some than to others. It is not the intention to rehash this issue here, merely to state that in keeping with the topic of this conference, in most libraries such fees are of marginal importance as income producers. Exceptions to this are the medical and law libraries where the level of fees set for everything from photocopies to information services makes them substantial sources of income. Most academic libraries have neither the desire nor the ability to exploit these revenue sources to this extent.

Whether such things as fines, interlibrary loan fees, book replacement charges, and other fees directly related to library services are significant factors will depend, in many cases, on institutional policy. For most academic libraries, these charges are either reimbursement for expenses or intended to achieve other objectives, that is, the return of books, than to raise funds.

As Poole and St. Clair (1986) state, "Libraries have never been, nor can they ever be, free. They are expensive to create and maintain, and, as their mission becomes increasingly tied to sophisticated automated systems, so their price accelerates."[7]

This places all the more financial pressure on us who are charged with keeping libraries modern and useful in the context of current information requirements. In the quest for adequate funds, local funding sources, other than direct institutional support, may not substantially close the gap, but they should not be overlooked.

NOTES

1. John M. Budd, "Academic Libraries: Institutional Support and Internal Expenditures," *Library Administration and Management*, 4(Summer 1990):154–158.

2. D. Selsky, "Academic Libraries: Increasingly Funded by Private Sources," *Library Journal,* 114(August 1989):38.

3. Association of Research Libraries. Office of Management Services. *Library Development and Fund Raising Capabilities,* SPEC Kit #146 (July–August 1988); summarized in accompanying *SPEC FLIER* containing cited figures and quotations.

4. Gregory H. Ritter, "Is Your Endowment Campaign to Be or Not to Be?," *Bottom Line,* 4(Winter 1990):13.

5. Susan Goldberg, "Starting a Development Office: One Academic Library's Experience. *Bottom Line,* 4(Summer 1990):31–33.

6. *Ibid.,* p. 32.

7. Jay Martin Poole and Gloriana St. Clair, "Funding Online Services from the Materials Budget." *College and Research Libraries,* 47(May 1986):225.

OTHER SOURCES

Beltran, Ann Bristow. "Funding Computer-Assisted Reference in Academic Research Libraries." *Journal of Academic Librarianship,* 13(March 1987):4–7.

Martin, Murray S. "Stagnant Budgets: Their Effects on Academic Libraries." *Bottom Line,* 3:3(1989):10–16.

Local Funding of Public Libraries: Critical Issues for the '90s

John D. Hales, Jr.
Director
Suwannee River Regional Library
Live Oak, Florida

I'm not sure I'm really the one to be sharing wisdom on local funding, since I'm the director who is having the Hamilton County Correctional Institution not make license plates, but rather construct a new county library. And last year I convinced Gilchrist County Commission that the new voting hall in Trenton, Florida, could be used as a public library the other 363 days or so a year that it was not a precinct house.

However, depending on whom you cite, local funding of public libraries is estimated at between 82 and 92 percent of the total budget. The differences appear to be that some sources include local non-governmental funds and some don't.

Recent *Library Journal* articles use the lower percentages, while Dean William Summers of Florida State University's School of Library and Information Studies, in a presentation on public library funding, quoted 81 percent, plus approximately another 11 percent from other funds.

Most local funds are from city, county, or municipality sales taxes, income taxes, or real estate taxes. They come from (a) general funds, (b) library tax levies, or (c) specially earmarked tax revenues.

Each year we must "justify" budget requests for a share of this general fund money. Of course, the effort to do so is increasing in complexity with the serious social issues that are confronting our funding bodies, such as indigent health care, criminal justice costs, solid waste disposal, and decaying infrastructure, especially roads.

What are the opportunities or the avenues to improve local funding from the general revenues, if they aren't tied to a funding formula?

Are you doing all you can do to tell the funding authority your story?

Do you include funding authorities in library mailings?

Do you have them come to the library?

Do you do an annual report that is of interest and relevant to their way of thinking?

Are you using the Output Measures of the Public Library Association to keep statistics, and do you use patterns that can aid in selling your budget and worth to the community?

Are you really using the board of your library Friends to the best advantage?

You can't sit back and say you've got 4 percent of the general funds. If you do, you will never *really* move your library through the critical 90's.

The second type of funding variation comes from real estate taxes levied specially for operation of the public library. The format and types vary greatly from state to state. In Florida in recent years several counties have become taxing districts and have passed referendums for tax districts. Some have been successful and some have not. In one of the most rapidly growing communities in the state, a referendum was defeated almost 5 to 1. The process for becoming a tax district requires sophisticated, thorough planning and good timing, timing, timing.

In the '90s the question regarding taxes based on real estate will have to consider carefully various parts of the country that have in recent years viewed property taxes as unjustifiably high and burdensome and have led to "taxpayer revolts: An Issues-Oriented Approach" as Verna Pungitore says in *Public Librarianship* (New York: Greenwood Press).

The third and less common source of revenues are intangible property taxes, local income taxes, and so on that are earmarked for library services. I could find very little movement in this direction in recent years.

It's obvious that by far the most critical revenue source for libraries in the '90s is local funding levels. Those of us who are competing for general fund revenues are being squeezed out, and I would venture to say will continue to be.

There are other ways beyond the basic tax dollar that libraries must actively pursue in the '90s. Although time consuming, difficult, and no panacea, the earmarking of funding sources for libraries seems to be the most critical issue.

Many of us now are involved in fund raising, as 68.3 percent of 269 libraries surveyed by the subcommittee of the Fundraising Development Section of LAMA in 1989 have been involved in fund raising in the last four years.

The good old book sale was the number one event; 106 libraries used that technique. Other methods such as lectures, mystery nights, fee-based services, musical events, book clubs, story hours, and such activities as direct mail, telephone solicitation, and door-to-door corporate requests were used.

These activities often are a lot of fun, help development community awareness, and build a broader base of constituency. But they can get stale, and there are always the ups and downs of volunteer commitments.

Friends Groups' activities such as bazaars, bake sales, symphony under the stars, basketball for books, and so on should be playing a part in local funding.

Daniel Bradbury of Kansas City says there must be 101 recipes for chocolate chip cookies. Each is a little different in taste, texture, and total result. The similarity is that most all *look* like chocolate chip cookies. Friends Groups, like chocolate chip cookies, can be put together in a wide variety of ways, using different recipes, and sometimes different ingredients, but they still are identifiable as Friends Groups.

They may or may not have nuts—just like some chocolate chip cookies, but they generally all have the betterment, promotion, and growth of the library at heart, and can be tremendously valuable.

Last year, for example, Friends raised over $1.5 million for Florida libraries. I think they are vastly underestimated, because their impact on state and local funding cannot really be measured. Leon County's new $10,000,000 library is the direct result of Friends' impact.

Another more widely used concept in recent years has been the effort to establish trusts and foundations, which can serve the purpose of facilitating recurring significant corporate or private donations to public libraries. The process of establishing the foundation legally and with IRS knowledge requires professional expertise. Legal counsel is a must. Active, knowledgeable, and well-connected board members should be appointed. Clear definitions for use of the revenues should be in place. Many libraries have hired an executive director who has fund-raising experience. Some involve the Friends organization and some don't.

In Broward County in 1986–1987, $1,000,000 was raised to begin a foundation. In Alma, Michigan, a $65,000 seed gift began an endowment that uses 80 percent of its earned interest to acquire materials. The other 20 percent is fed back into the principal.

The integrity of the foundation is very important; you must make sure that funds are targeted solely for the library, if the city or county is involved in the process. Remember to emphasize *supplement* not *supplant* to all who are involved in the process.

The major issue relating to obtaining funding from private sources, or for that matter the use of volunteers, is that your local funding body will consciously or unconsciously think that the funds or sources can be used in lieu of local funds for the provision of basic services. As a result, many librarians and trustees don't even examine "outside sources," but I think that's a mistake. Others emphasize fund-raising efforts as limited to so-called extras.

In Dallas, Patrick O'Brien learned a bitter lesson. The second year after establishing an endowment, the city, he learned, had treated the income as a credit on the budget. The wording was hazy enough so that city finance officers could pull off the credit move. In O'Brien's next fund-raising effort to enhance the children's area, he was certain that the funds were not included in his regular funding structure.

Because of this concept, there is the "damned if you do, damned if you don't" aspect of fund-raising. The politicians or citizens who see the success that may come from outside fund-raising activities may not see the value of a commitment of tax dollars to a library, such as Boston's, that has a $10,000,000 trust fund. The diminishing of the local government's sense of public need can become a serious consequence.

As a postscript to endowments or trusts, I offer the thoughts of Jeffrey Krull of Allen County Public Library of Fort Wayne, Indiana. He believes that endowments sometimes are difficult to fund, the reason being that many foundations are themselves endowments, and feel their money should be used to fund specific projects and purchases, and not to set up more endowments. Krull suggests that one must be clear that endowment income or revenues are used for specific purposes.

Local funding in the '90s probably cannot be discussed (no matter what your personal opinion is) without mentioning fees. The sister, or sinister persona of fees is always present. Opponents or proponents are being steadily driven, by their funding bodies, local desire for service, or even peer pressure, to make hard decisions regarding fees.

There is the basic philosophy to maintain the public library's fundamental mission of equal access to information, or "free" library service. Ron Dubberly is a staunch supporter of no fees; he feels that a fee-based library would ultimately reduce the spectrum of ideas and information to the public.

Charlie Robinson, on the other hand, says in his usual eloquent manner, "Hogwash, there is no equal access. When you take into account distance, time, parking, materials selection, budget size variations, and so forth, there is never going to be equal access, it's unrealistic."

There are those who are in a quandary, such as Linda Crismond, executive director of ALA, whose personal opinion is that "fees are inevitable"; our bosses want it, our colleagues in museums and parks suggest it is appropriate, and our customers often are willing to pay for expensive, unusual, or specialized services. Of course, the ALA's position on fees, adopted in 1977, strongly denounced them as a form of discrimination.

No matter what your position or your funding body, it is more likely that fees will be even more of an issue in the '90s than in the past. As we examine local funding, the community library and its mission and goals will become a criterion for examining this alternative.

In Giacoma's thorough *The Fee or Free Decision*, he also links ethnic makeup, socioeconomic composition, political party affiliation, and even the form of local government as factors that will contribute to fee or free decision-making processes.

In growth states, or expanding urban areas, local funding may be augmented by impact fees. In areas where the impact of new shopping areas creates changing traffic patterns and new residential areas, or in the establishment of planned living communities, impact fees associated with new construction have generally proved worthwhile.

In Florida a few counties and municipalities have impact fees that are earmarked for libraries. In fact, one South Florida library director told me last year that he had so much impact fee revenue, spending it was causing him a problem—a nice local funding problem.

Most of the local revenue from tax or private sources I have discussed has dealt primarily with operating costs. Bond issues have played important roles at local levels in providing buildings, furniture, and materials for libraries throughout the nation. Most bond issues must be voted on by the communities. Bond issues have provided new libraries and been the means of developing systems in urban and suburban centers. They require an intensive education campaign, a good analysis of the political climate, and an undying commitment from supporters. It can generally be assumed that many will say it can't be done. There isn't enough time and bond issues always fail. However, in fact, most well-planned and thorough bond issues pass.

In sum, the critical issues of the '90s appear little different from those of the '80s. Local funding will continue to be dependent predominantly on local tax dollars. The outside realistic funding sources will need to be more enthusiastically examined, especially those that can lead to recurring revenues.

We all will need to do a better job in proving the worth of libraries, as we try to provide more and more services even with shrinking local budgets.

Pat Woodrum tells this story about fund raising: "Following hurricane *Alicia*, rescue workers tediously made their way into an area that had been almost totally devastated by the tragic storm. They worked for hours to remove the debris that had virtually buried a mobile home. Finally they were able to reach the front door, and knocking loudly, called out, 'This is the Red Cross.' All was quiet for a moment, then a voice from within replied, 'We've had some problems lately. I don't think we'll be able to contribute much this year.' "

Librarians, like the Red Cross, know a number of faithful followers who will support improving or at least holding onto positions in the community. We must continue to provide the efficient service we've provided in the past and examine all alternatives of assistance, because I have the forecast—and it calls for more hurricanes.

BIBLIOGRAPHY: SUGGESTED ADDITIONAL READING

Introduction: Library Funding and the Concept of Federalism

Advisory Commission on Intergovernmental Relations. *General Review Sharing: An ACIR Re-Evaluation.* Washington, DC: ACIR, 1974.

Advisory Commission on Intergovernmental Relations. *The Intergovernmental Grant System: An Assessment and Proposed Policies.* Washington, DC: ACIR, 1978.

Breivik, Patricia Senn, and Gibson, E. Barr. *Funding Alternatives for Libraries.* Chicago: American Library Association, 1979.

Caputo, David A. "General Revenue Sharing and Federalism." In *The Annuals of the American Academy of Political and Social Science*, 130–142. Philadelphia: American Academy of Political and Social Science, 1975.

Cohen, Nina T. "External Contracting for Library Services." In *Financing Information Services: Problems, Changing Approaches, and New Opportunities for Academic and Research Libraries*, edited by Peter Spyers-Duran and Thomas W. Mann, Jr., 154–164. Westport, CT: Greenwood Press, 1985.

Frase, Robert W. *Library Funding and Public Support: A Working Paper on the Background and Issues.* Chicago: American Library Association, 1973.

Getz, Malcolm. *Public Libraries: An Economic View.* Baltimore: Johns Hopkins University Press, 1980.

Goridy, Frank William. "General Revenue Sharing and Public Libraries: An Estimate of Fiscal Impact." *Library Journal*, 52(1):1–20.

Govan, James F. "The Creeping Invisible Hand: Entrepreneurial Librarianship," *Library Journal* (January 1988):35–38.

Kaufman, Paula. "A Crisis in Scholarly Publication—Serials Price Escalation and New Title Proliferation." *Information Issues* (Fall 1989): 1–4.

Lynch, Mary Jo. *Non-tax Sources of Revenue for Public Libraries: ALA*

Survey Report, ALA Office for Research and Office for Library Personnel Resources. Chicago: American Library Association, 1988.

McCain, Roger A. "Information as Property and as a Public Good: Perspectives from the Economic Theory of Property Rights." *Library Quarterly*, 58(3):265–282.

Minasian, Jora A. "Television Pricing and the Theory of Public Goods." *Journal of Law & Economics*, 7(October 1964):71–80.

National Commission on Libraries and Information Science. *Evaluation of the Effectiveness of Federal Funding of Public Libraries: A Study Prepared for NCLIS by Government Studies and Systems, Inc., Philadelphia, PA.* Washington, DC: NCLIS, 1976.

Niskanen, William A. "Bureaucrats and Politicians." *Journal of Law & Economics*, 18(December 1975):617–643.

Pavlovsky, Lilia. "Timing it Right: How Librarians Can Influence the Federal Budget." *The Bottom Line*, 4(2):10–13.

Part 1: Federal Funding of Academic and Public Libraries

Advanced Commission in Intergovernmental Relations. *Categorical Grants: Their Role and Design.* Washington, DC: ACIR, 1977.

American Library Association. *ALA Federal Legislative Policy.* Chicago: American Library Association, 1987.

Federal Grants for Library and Information Services: A Selective Guide. Washington, DC: American Library Association, 1991.

Washington Newsletter. Washington, DC: American Library Association.

Association of College and Research Libraries, ACRL Legislation Committee. "Higher Education Act Reauthorization." *College and Research Libraries News*, 51(September 1990):716–721.

Bob, Murray L. "Confessions of a Grantsperson." *Library Journal* (June 15, 1988):26–29.

Bush, George. *America 2000: An Education Strategy Sourcebook.* Washington, DC: Department of Education, 1991.

Hernon, Peter, and McClure, Charles. *Federal Information Policies in the 1980's: Conflicts and Issues.* Norwood, NJ: Ablex, 1987.

Kranich, Nancy. "Government Information: Less is Dangerous." *Thought and Action: The NEA Higher Education Journal*, 4(Spring 1988): 37–48. Reprinted in Jane Anne Hannigan, *The Best of Library Literature, 1988*, Metuchen, NJ: Scarecrow Press, 1989.

———"Information Drought: Next Crisis for the American Farmer?" *Library Journal*, 114(June 15, 1989):22–27. Reprinted in Jane Anne

Hannigan, *The Best of Library Literature, 1989*, 190–204. Metuchen, NJ: Scarecrow Press, 1990.

Mason, Marilyn Gell. *The Federal Role in Library and Information Services*. White Plains, NY: Knowledge Industry Publications, 1983.

National Commission on Libraries and Information Science. *Alternatives for Financing the Public Library*. Washington, DC: National Commission on Libraries and Information Science, 1974.

Parkhurst, Carol A., ed. *Library Perspectives on NREN: The National Research on Education Network*. Chicago: Library and Information Technology Association, 1990.

Trezza, Alphonse F. "Federal Funding Alternatives: A Theme Conference Summary. Based on Prospects, Possibilities and Alternatives for Federal Support of Libraries and Information Services." White House Conference on Libraries and Information Services, preconference meetings on special themes, June 8–9 and September 14, 1978. Washington, DC: National Commission on Libraries and Information Science, 1979.

U.S. Congress, House of Representatives, Committee on Education and Labor, Subcommittee on Select Education. *Preliminary Staff Report on Educational Research, Development, and Dissemination: Reclaiming a Vision for the 1990's and Beyond*. Washington, DC: Government Printing Office, 1988.

U.S. Library of Congress, Congressional Research Service. "Federal Assistance to Libraries: Current Programs and Issues." Washington, DC: Library of Congress, 1990.

Part 2: State Funding of Academic and Public Libraries

ACADEMIC LIBRARIES

Blumenstyle, Goldie, and Cage, Mary Crystal. "Public Colleges Expect Financial Hardships in 1991." *Chronicles of Higher Education* (January 1):1.

Gregory, Vicki L. "Library Cooperative Programs and Coordinating Agencies of Higher Education." *Library and Information Science Research*, 10(July 1988):316–317.

Jefferson, Thomas. Letter to Charles Yancey, 1816.

LaCroix, Michael J. *Minitex and Illinet: Two Library Networks*. Urbana: University of Illinois Graduate School of Library and Information Science, Occasional Papers (178).

Medina, Sue. Letter to Don Hardy, 1991.

———"Network of Alabama Academic Libraries: An Emerging State Network." *The Southeastern Librarian* (Summer 1987):41.

Mooney, Carolyn J. "Financial Stresses Hit Professors, But Most Colleges Protect Tenured Ranks." *Chronicles of Higher Education* (February 27):A1.

Okerson, Ann, and Kendon, Stubbs. "The Library Doomsday Machine." *Publisher's Weekly* (February 8, 1991):36.

Osborne, David. "Keynote Speech: The Role of Information in the Economy of the Southeast." *Southeastern Librarian* (Summer 1990): 57.

Potter, William Gray. "Collection Overlap in the LCS Network in Illinois." *Library Quarterly* (April 1986):119–141.

Sloane, Bernard G., and Stewart, David J. "Illinet Online: Enhancing and Expanding Access to Library Resources in Illinois." *Library HiTech*, 6(1988):95–101.

"Special LJ Roundup: The Fiscal Fate of the States." *Library Journal* (January 1991):36.

Toffler, Alvin. *Power Shift*. New York: Bantam Books, 1990.

Wanninger, Patricia Dwyer. "The Sound and the Fury of RFP." *Library Journal* (December 1990):87–89.

PUBLIC LIBRARIES

Advanced Commission in Intergovernmental Relations. *The Property Tax in a Changing Environment: Selected State Studies,* Washington, DC: ACIR, 1974.

Boyer, Richard, and David, Sayageau. *Places Rated Almanac: Your Guide to Finding the Best Places to Live in America.* 2nd ed. Chicago: Rand McNally, 1985.

Curry, Elizabeth A., and Whittler, Susan Sellers, eds. *Florida Public Library Board Manual, 1988.* Tallahassee: State Library of Florida, 1988.

"Legislative Alert." *Florida Libraries* 34(February 1991):6–12.

National Commission on Libraries and Information Science. *Improving State and Public Libraries: Report Prepared by the Urban Libraries Council by the Governor's Studies and Systems, Inc., Philadelphia, PA.* Washington, DC: NCLIS, 1977.

Prentice, Ann E. *Public Library Finance,* Chicago: American Library Association, 1977.

Trezza, Alphonse F. *Sources of Funding for Public Libraries.* Binghamton, NY: Haworth Press, 1989.

————*Standards and Guidelines for Florida Public Library Services*. Winter Park, FL: Florida Library Association, 1985.

Tripplett, Glenn, and Terrie, E. Walter. *1990 Florida Library Directory with Statistics*. Tallahassee: Florida Department of State, Division of Library and Information Services, 1990.

Wheeler, Joseph L., and Goldhor, Herbert. *Practical Administration of Public Libraries*. New York: Harper & Row, 1962.

Part 3: Samuel Lazerow Memorial Lecture

Carrigan, Dennis P. "Librarians and the 'Dismal Science.' " *Library Journal* (June 15, 1988):22–25.

McCain, Roger A. "Information as Property and as a Public Good: Perspectives from the Economic Theory of Property Rights." *Library Quarterly*, (July 1988):265–282.

Schuman, Patricia Glass. "The Image of Librarians: Substance or Shadow?" *The Journal of Academic Librarianship*, 16(May 1990):86–89.

————"Making the Case for Access: American Library Association Needs You." *RQ*, 29(Winter 1989):166–172.

————"Reclaiming Our Technological Future." *Library Journal*, 115(March 1, 1990):34–38.

Part 4: Local Funding of Academic and Public Libraries

ACADEMIC LIBRARIES

Association of Research Libraries. Office of Management Services. *Library Development and Fund Raising Capabilities*, SPEC Kit #146 (July–August 1988).

Beltran, Ann Bristow. "Funding Computer-Assisted Reference in Academic Research Libraries." *Journal of Academic Librarianship*, 13(March 1987):4–7.

Budd, John M. "Academic Libraries: Institutional Support and Internal Expenditures." *Library Administration and Management*, 4(Summer 1990):154–158.

Goldberg, Susan. "Starting a Development Office: One Academic Library's Experience." *Bottom Line*, 4(Summer 1990):31–33.

Martin, Murray S. "Stagnant Budgets: Their Effects on Academic Libraries." *Bottom Line*, 3(Summer 1989):10–16.

Poole, Jay Martin, and St. Clair, Gloriana. "Funding Online Services from the Materials Budget." *College and Research Libraries,* 47(May 1986):225–229.

Ritter, Gregory H. "Is Your Endowment Campaign to Be or Not to Be?" *Bottom Line,* 4(Winter 1990):11–13.

Selsky, D. "Academic Libraries: Increasingly Funded by Private Sources." *Library Journal,* 114(August 1989):38.

PUBLIC LIBRARIES

Bonnell, Pamela G. *Fund Raising for the Small Library.* Chicago: American Library Association, 1982. (Small Libraries Publication no. 8)

Geddes, Andrew. *Fiscal Responsibilities and the Small Public Library.* Chicago: American Library Association, 1978. (Small Libraries Publication no. 3)

Giacoma, Pete. "User Fees: Pros and Cons." *Bottom Line,* 3(Winter 1989):27–30.

————*The Fee of Free Decision: Legal, Economic, Political, and Ethical Perspectives for Public Libraries.* New York: Neal Schuman, 1990.

Intner, Sheila S., and Schement, Jorge R. "The Ethic of Free Service." *Library Journal,* 112(October 1, 1987):50–52.

Krull, Jeffrey R. "Private Dollar$ for Public Libraries." *Library Journal* (January 1991):65–68.

Lemov, Penelope. "User Fees, Once the Answer to City Budget Prayers, May Have Reached Their Peak." *Governing* (March 1989): 24–30.

Prentice, Anne E. *Financial Planning for Libraries.* Metuchen, NJ: Scarecrow Press, 1983.

Trezza, Alphonse F. "Sources of Funding for Public Libraries in Managing Public Libraries in the 21st Century." *Journal of Library Administration,* 11(1989):67–80.